MARITIME LONDON

MARITIME LONDON

An Historical Journey in Pictures and Words

Anthony Burton

PEN & SWORD
TRANSPORT

AN IMPRINT OF PEN & SWORD BOOKS LTD.
YORKSHIRE – PHILADELPHIA

First published in Great Britain in 2022 by
Pen and Sword Transport
An imprint of
Pen & Sword Books Ltd.
Yorkshire - Philadelphia

ISBN 978 1 39909 287 6

A CIP catalogue record for this book is available from the British Library.

Typeset by SJmagic DESIGN SERVICES, India.
Printed and bound in India by Replika Press Pvt. Ltd.

Pen & Sword Books Ltd incorporates the imprints of Pen & Sword Books Archaeology, Atlas, Aviation, Battleground, Discovery, Family History, History, Maritime, Military, Naval, Politics, Railways, Select, Transport, True Crime, Fiction, Frontline Books, Leo Cooper, Praetorian Press, Seaforth Publishing, Wharncliffe and White Owl.

For a complete list of Pen & Sword titles please contact

PEN & SWORD BOOKS LIMITED
47 Church Street, Barnsley, South Yorkshire, S70 2AS, England
E-mail: enquiries@pen-and-sword.co.uk
Website: www.pen-and-sword.co.uk

or

PEN AND SWORD BOOKS
1950 Lawrence Rd, Havertown, PA 19083, USA
E-mail: Uspen-and-sword@casematepublishers.com
Website: www.penandswordbooks.com

CONTENTS

INTRODUCTION

When writing about London in an historical context, there is always something of a dilemma. Which London is one talking about – the original city of London, scarcely larger than a village, or the massive sprawl that is the new Greater London? As this book is about maritime life, the main emphasis is going to be on the tidal River Thames. This sets the westward limit at Teddington lock, where the jurisdiction passes from the Port of London Authority to the Thames Conservancy. I have chosen Barking Creek as the eastern limit, as that will include the whole area occupied by the old London docks. Although the word 'maritime' is usually taken as being connected specifically to the sea, which is not a problem with regard to the activities on the tideway, I have also extended the scope to include other forms of water transport that have served the capital over the years. The illustration below shows Wenceslaus Hollar's view of the Thames from Bankside in 1647 and shows most of the river that will be featured over the following pages.

A panoramic view of the Thames in the seventeenth century by Wenceslaus Hollar (1607-77). It shows the contrast between the shipping below London Bridge and small craft upstream. The original picture was 5 metres long.

CHAPTER 1

BEGINNINGS

The Thames lies at the heart of London's very existence and its maritime life. It is reasonable to assume that it was being used for transport long before the settlement on the river got its present name. A lot of what happened in the distant past has to be speculative. When did *Homo Sapiens* first take to the water? It is easy to imagine a stone age man seeing a floating log and realizing that if he held on to it, he could cross a river. He might have been even more adventurous and tried sitting on it, but as any kid who has played around on water can tell you, the phrase 'easy as falling off a log' has real meaning. He could have made something altogether more stable by lashing several logs together to form a raft. Archaeologists believe that the only way in which the blue stones at Stonehenge could have been brought to the site from their quarry in the Preseli Hills of Wales was round the coast by raft and then up the River Avon, past the present site of Salisbury, to a point as close as possible to the henge. Perhaps the simplest craft, other than a raft, would have been a log boat. With the use of fire and basic tools it would be possible to hollow out a log and give it a boat shape. Sitting *in* a log would be a lot safer than sitting *on* it. All this is speculation, but when we come to look at the Bronze Age, we have actual physical evidence of what can be called boats.

In 1880, in the mud on the north bank of the Humber at North Ferriby, the shifting mud revealed what appeared to be the remains of an ancient boat, but no one did very much about it until half a century later when two brothers, E.V. and C.W. Wright, set out to investigate the site and began the tricky job of excavation. It was not simply that the timbers were encased in cloying mud that made the work difficult, but the site was submerged at every high tide. The brothers, with the help of a few volunteers, had a maximum of just five hours between tides to remove the remains. They started work in 1938, but they were only able to remove three sections that were stored in the family greenhouse before war broke out and everything came to a halt. E.V. Wright was able to do a little more work when he came home on leave in 1940, and while clearing away the two ends of the boat, discovered a second, similar vessel alongside.

In 1946 work could restart and this time an attempt was made to release boat number one from its muddy grave by sliding boiler plates underneath the clay and dragging the whole thing above the high-water mark. Things seemed to be going well, but as they were manoeuvring it onto solid land, the whole vessel collapsed into fragments. The pieces were then carefully laid out, numbered and work began on trying to fit the jigsaw together again. Unfortunately, little remains of this work, but with boat number two there was rather more success, though again it was a question of reassembling fragments, but conservation techniques proved more successful. In 1963, a third boat was discovered on the same site. A splendid reconstruction of the site and a vessel can be seen in the National Maritime Museum at Greenwich. The vessels have been dated to the Bronze Age, around 1500 BCE.

Enough remains to show a great deal about the vessels and how they were constructed. The boat that has been best preserved measured roughly 13 metres. At the base of the vessel was the keel, a timber that runs from stem to stern. As this is too long for a single timber, two sections had to be fastened together by means of a scarf joint. Instead of the ends abutting directly together, the two ends that are to meet are partly cut away, so that they can overlap each other, and then be pinned. This technique has been used for the keels of wooden ships for centuries: if you are ever fortunate enough to get right down to the bottom of the hull of H.M.S. *Victory* you will find a neat scarf on the keel. The two timbers of the Bronze Age keel were carved from solid oak and given a slight upward curve at either end.

The base of the vessel was built up using thinner planks that had been carved and fitted together, rather like a tongue and groove. There were no nails, instead, the planks were sewn together with strips of yew, and then made watertight by filling the gaps with moss and then covering them with slats. The sides were extended upwards by pairs of planks – the strakes – and cleats were found on the keel, to which cross battens could

The third of the North Ferriby Bronze Age boats during excavation from the mud of the Humber.

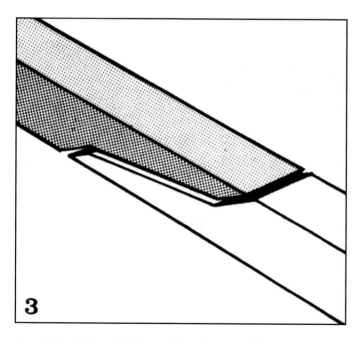

A scarf joint; joints of this type have been used for connecting the timbers to form the keel of a wooden ship for literally thousands of years.

be added to strengthen the floor. Marks on the timber suggest that at least two different tools were used in shaping the timber, one with a straight blade and one curved. Because the boats were incomplete, we have no way of knowing how many strakes were originally used to build up the sides or the exact shape of the finished boats. There is another obvious question that needs answering; were these vessels unique to this region or were similar vessels also to be found in the south of England and possibly on the Thames? The question received a partial answer in 1992 when another Bronze Age vessel was discovered during road works near Dover. The vessel was of a similar age to the North Ferriby boats but was far more complete.

This time, the vessel was cut into sections for removal, and then reassembled. The surviving portion was 9.5 metres long and appears to be about two thirds of the total length – making it comparable to the Ferriby boats – and the construction is similar. However, enough remained to produce a half-sized replica that was built

The excavated remains of the Bronze Age boat found near Dover and now on display in the Dover Museum.

using the same construction technique and materials as the original and was given an outing in Falmouth Harbour, where it proved quite manageable. Most experts believe that the vessel could have been sea-going, in which case it seems even more likely that there was a busy maritime trade round the south east coast of Britain 2,500 years ago, and that must have included the Thames. The remains of the original boat are now in the Dover Museum.

Because so few boats from prehistory have survived, there are vast gaps in our knowledge of what would have been in use on our rivers at any particular period. The next major find takes us out of the Bronze Age and into the Iron Age, that lasted from around 500 BCE until the first Roman invasion. This was a period from which several log boats have been recovered. Most have been very modest craft, basically canoes, but others have been immense vessels of more complex construction. The largest craft yet is the Hasholme log boat, discovered at Holme-on-Spalding

Moor in East Yorkshire in 1984. The vessel is almost 13 metres long, 1.4 metres maximum beam. The log is oak, and it has been estimated that the original log from which it was made would have to have been at least 14 metres long and over 5 metres wide. That is a massive timber and must have weighed getting on for 30 tons. Bringing the log to the construction site and manhandling it once it was there would have been a complex and difficult operation. The boat has a flat bottom, but curves toward the bow, which is closed off by separate timbers, while the stern is closed by a single timber set at right angles to the hull, what would now be known as a transom stern. This is a substantial craft, which has no indication of ever having had a mast, so it has been estimated that it would have needed a crew of eighteen at least to move it through the water. A second equally grand log boat was later found in Poole Harbour, so it is clear that craft of this kind were in use in different parts of the country, again almost certainly including the Thames.

The Iron Age log boat found at Holme-on-Spalding and now in the Hull and East Riding Museum.

So far, there has been a large amount of supposition about the maritime life of the Thames in prehistoric times, but with the arrival of the Romans we finally have firm evidence of what was happening, and, of course, we have the beginnings of the city of London, with the foundation of Londinium between 47 and 50 CE. It was established at an important crossing point on the Thames, the first to be reached when coming in from the sea. But a mere decade later there was a major rebellion. When the king of the Iceni died without leaving a male heir, the Romans, who forbade female inheritance, simply took over his land and wealth. His daughter Boudica protested, and the Romans had her flogged and her daughters raped. The outrage led to a major uprising led by Boudica herself, which resulted in the Romans abandoning Londinium, which was then razed to the ground. Ultimately, the rebellion failed, and the Romans began rebuilding the city and establishing it as a major port.

Serious archaeological excavation of the Roman port began in the 1970s, when it was discovered that the waterfront in the first century was approximately 100 metres north of the present line. The dock area lay within what is now the City of London, just to the north of Lower Thames Street. The excavation revealed that the quays had been constructed with immense oak timbers, up to 9 metres long and 600 mm by 400 mm in cross section. These were piled in stacks up to nine metres high to create the quay wall, and the space behind was infilled with clay and gravel. The timbers have been dated to within the period from the first to the third centuries. There is evidence that the construction work was carried out by the military, as the ends of timbers were stamped with official marks, and sections of armour and part of a leather tent were found on site. There was also evidence of warehouse buildings along the quay, at Miles Lane and Pudding Lane. These were substantial buildings; one at Miles Lane was built of stone, 35 metres long and 9 metres wide, with several rooms, the largest of which faced out onto the river.

There was a large landing stage, built c.70 CE, near the present Pudding Lane, that may have been used as a ferry pier before the first bridge across the river was completed some fifteen to twenty years later. The wharf area was regularly extended along the river into the third century. As heavy stones, weighing up to a ton, have been found in Roman shipwrecks, there must have been some sort of crane available to lift them from the hold, but no direct evidence has been found. However, we do know from Roman ports on the Mediterranean that they did use cranes, so there is no reason why they could not have been used here – and it is difficult to see how the ships could have been unloaded without some sort of lifting device.

We know quite a lot about the goods that passed through the port of Londinium. One reason that the Romans bothered with this group of islands off the coast of mainland Europe was their well-known mineral wealth. They mined for gold in Wales, iron ore in the Forest of Dean and lead in the Mendips. Three stamped lead ingots were recovered from an excavated London warehouse site. The Romans also imported what they would have regarded as essentials, but were unobtainable in Britain, such as amphorae of olive oil from Spain and barrels of wine from Southern France, remains of which have been found. Large quantities of broken pottery were discovered that had never been used, that had been imported from Gaul and could have been broken in transit. The idea that trade with Gaul was important was reinforced by the discovery of an inscription from the second century, that names one Tiberinius Celerianus as being a London merchant, who came from Bellovaci, near present day Beauvais. There would have been far more items traded, many of them perishable and leaving few if any traces. One unsavoury trade has, however, been recorded in London; a slave girl called Fortunata was sold in London for 600 denarii.

We have a picture of a busy port, extending down a considerable length along the north bank of the Thames and trading in a wide variety of goods. And, thanks to discoveries that began in the twentieth century, we know a great deal about the ships in which the goods were carried. The first discovery was made in 1910, when work began on excavating the foundations for the new County Hall. Only the centre of the vessel had survived, but it was a substantial portion, 13 metres long and 5.5 metres wide. The construction was entirely of oak, and unlike most early vessels was carvel built, with the planks abutting each other edge to edge, held together by mortice and tenon joints. At the bottom of the boat was the keel to which the other planks were attached by oak treenails – a form of wooden peg. The collapsed side suggested that it originally rose to a height of 1.55 metres, with a deck 1.3 metres above the bottom. The remains were held for a time in the London Museum, but disintegrated. Fortunately, a careful drawing had been made at the time, showing exactly how it was laid out when first discovered (below).

The next ship to be discovered was found in the bed of the Thames at Blackfriars in 1962. Where the County Hall vessel had simply been abandoned, this one had obviously sunk as it still contained its cargo of building stone and a partially shaped millstone. A votive offering of a bronze coin was dated to around 88 CE. Unlike the first vessel, there was no keel, but two keel plans and although it was also of carvel construction, this vessel used iron nails with conical heads, instead of treenails. She was probably around 14 metres long and 6.5 metres wide with a cargo hold in the centre, roofed by oak planks. A rectangular slot where the mast would have been stepped was about a third of the way from the bows. She was constructed from oak, most probably built in Britain and experiments suggest that the vessel was capable of sea voyages and of carrying a cargo

of around 50 tonnes. This was clearly a substantial merchantman.

A quite different vessel was discovered in 1958, while work was being done on preparing the foundations for a new surgical wing for Guy's Hospital. One end survived, and was sharply pointed, but otherwise construction of the hull was not basically dissimilar to the Blackfriars ship. The hull has been estimated at 11 metres long and 4.25 metres beam, but the significant fact was the height of the sides, a modest 0.5 metres. This means that she would have been totally unsuited for sea voyages and must have been used as a barge on the Thames. She was built in the second century and it has been established that the vessel was definitely built in Britain.

The Roman port continued to expand over the years and Londinium was busy with vessels of all kinds. There must have been far more different types of ship on the water than have been revealed by excavation. We know, for example, from the physical evidence that large quantities of fish were eaten, such

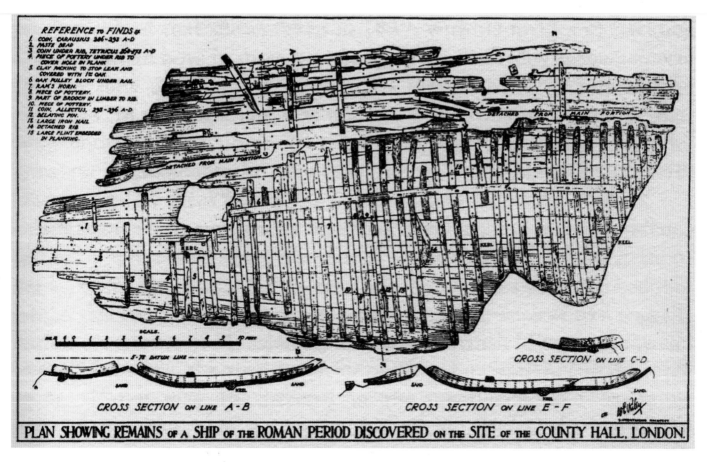

This diagram was drawn to show the remains of the Roman ship discovered during the building of County Hall, London; the remains later disintegrated.

A drawing made of the representation of a second century Roman ship carved on a sarcophagus in the Lateran Museum, Rome. It shows the typical square sail and prominent steer board.

as herring, so there must also have been a sizeable fishing fleet. And the Romans would certainly have had warships ready for use. Then, in the early fourth century, it all came to an end. The Romans withdrew from Britain and a new period of British history and the story of London began.

There is little written evidence for exactly when the Angles and Saxons began to move into Britain, but archaeology provides some interesting clues. Artefacts found in Roman cemeteries in the Thames valley indicate that Germanic mercenaries were employed in the area. They seem to have been based at a garrison at Mucking near the mouth of the Thames, for example. Perhaps they stayed on and encouraged others to follow them. That is only speculation, but what is clear is that London as a city simply ceased to exist, though the Roman walls survived. Remains of a Saxon farm were found on what had been the Roman city. But by the end of the Anglo-Saxon period, however, it seems that a new port had been established upstream of the original Roman quays. Around the year 1000, documents laid out the charges on vessels using the port – one penny for a large ship, one halfpenny for a small.

There are only two vessels discovered by archaeologists from this period. The first was the Sutton Hoo ship burial, found near Woodbridge in Suffolk in 1939 by a local archaeologist, Basil Brown, who undertook the excavation with Lieutenant-Commander J.K.D. Hutchinson of the Science Museum, London. The vessel had been covered by an earth mound and immense treasures were discovered, but of the ship itself, only a ghostly image remained in the sand; the wood had disintegrated and rotted. All the details were recorded in photos and drawings, but further work was put on hold by the outbreak of war. It was decided to reinvestigate the site in the 1960s, but when the archaeologists arrived, they found a woeful sight. The army had been there, dug a slit trench right through the burial mound, and trundled Bren-gun carriers all over it. Much of the early detail had been lost. However, a lot could be deduced from the earlier records and what had survived. This was an open rowing boat, 27.5 metres long by 4.25 metres beam. It had a keel plank, built up with nine strakes to each side. It was clinker built, with

The sandy outline of the great Anglo-Saxon ship found under a burial mound at Sutton Hoo.

The Sutton Hoo ship was buried with a great treasure hoard, demonstrating the craftsmanship of the period. This helmet is a particularly fine example.

the planks overlapping each other and held together by iron rivets. The hull was strengthened with 26 heavy wooden frames. The gunwale above the hull had claw holds to take up to twenty oars. There were separate stem and stern posts and steering was via a board set near the stern to the right of the vessel looking towards the bows. This became common practice. To avoid damaging the board, the vessel would normally be berthed with the opposite side against the quay. The two sides became known as the steer-board side, later changed to starboard, and the port side. A reconstruction of the site and the excavated ship can be seen at the National Maritime Museum, Greenwich.

The Sutton Hoo ship with its horde of golden treasures was used as the grave of a very high-ranking individual. Given the value of the grave goods found on site, the ship would have been carefully chosen as befitting his status. We cannot assume that every craft of this general type was built to the same high standard. The next major Anglo-Saxon discovery was a much more mundane vessel, an ordinary cargo ship. The vessel was discovered in the mud at Graveney in Kent in 1970. It was both shorter and tubbier than the Sutton Hoo ship – from the remains it was estimated to have been around 13.6 metres long, 4 metres wide and 1 metre high amidships. It was made of oak, clinker built, with a flat keel, and with the strakes held together with iron rivets. It might have had a mast, but that is not certain. The remains found in the hull show that at some time it carried loads of hops and stone for querns, hand operated devices for grinding grain. It was not suited for heavy seas but could have made short coastal voyages. One can easily imagine it delivering its load of hops to London brewers. As with other vessels described above, there is now a display in the museum at Greenwich.

The Graveney boat has been dated to the latter part of the tenth century, a time when London had regained some of its former importance as a port. But by the following century, everything was about to change with the Norman invasion and British history entered a new phase.

THE SAILING SHIP

From the time of the Norman conquest until the time of the Tudors, we no longer have direct physical evidence to tell us what ships were like. But there are enough illustrations and carvings to give us a good idea – even if some of them are remarkably primitive. Our first glimpse of the sort of ships that the Normans brought with them to British waters comes from the famous Bayeux tapestry. This extraordinary work can be thought of as the original strip cartoon. For those who have only seen reproductions of some parts, it comes as a shock to see the real thing, for it really is a narrow, embroidered strip, just 50 cm wide, but stretching out for almost 70 metres. The part that is of special interest here occurs near the beginning and shows the Norman

fleet crossing the Channel. These vessels are clearly part of the existing northern Europe tradition, with high sweeping prow and stern post, steer board and a single square-rigged mast. The first big change came probably at some time in the thirteenth century. A carving in Winchester Cathedral appears to show a vessel in which the steer board has been replaced by a rudder, attached by hinges to the stern post and worked by a tiller.

Warships of the early period had developed very distinct characteristics. They were designed to carry soldiers who would do the actual fighting and were built with fighting castles, superstructures built above the hull. Usually there was one aft, one forward and often a third, mounted on the single mast. The rather

William I's fleet on its way to England from the Bayeux Tapestry. The helmsman is controlling both the steer board and the single square sail.

bloodthirsty illustration (below) gives a good idea of how these castles were used in battle. The vessels are of the type known as cogs. Basically, they were designed in exactly the same way as the cogs used for trade, apart from the addition of the fighting castles. All that changed with the introduction of gunpowder from China in the fourteenth century and the introduction of guns. Warships would no longer simply be transports to take fighting men into battle but would fight naval battles with their armament. Up to this time, the sailors had simply managed the job of handling the ship, leaving it to others to do the actual fighting; now they would take on a new role as fighting sailors. The fighting castles disappeared, though the forecastle became the fo'c'sle, an area in the bows with crew accommodation, and the after castle was lowered to become the poop deck.

The square sail was ubiquitous in northern water for centuries, but in the Mediterranean, there was a quite different tradition, using triangular – lateen – sails, set on spars that were hung at roughly 45° to the mast. In Portugal, the caravel was developed with up to three masts, each with a lateen sail. It was in a vessel such as this that Columbus set sail for the East. It was not long, however, before it was recognised that the lateen sail and the square sail had complementary advantages. The former made for greater manoeuvrability; the latter provided greater driving force. The caravel was adapted into the caravel redonda, which now had square sails on the foremast, lateen on the main and mizzen. The advantages of such a system found their way to English shipbuilders and reached a new stage of development with the galleon. Typically, this would

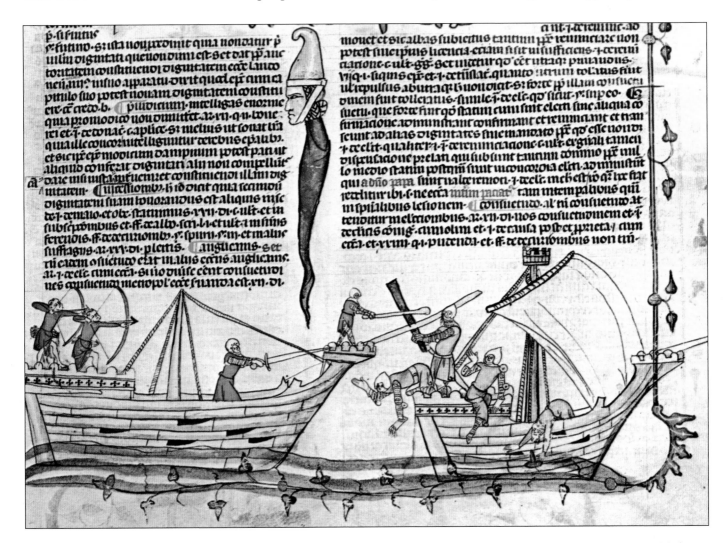

A medieval sea battle, showing the aft castle being used by archers and the forecastle for soldiers engaged in hand-to-hand fighting. From a fourteenth century manuscript.

be a four masted vessel, with square sails on the two fore masts and lateen on the two aft, and a further square sail set on the bowsprit. It was just such a vessel that Henry VIII ordered to be built at the Woolwich dockyard on the Thames between 1512 and 1514, the *Henri Grace á Dieu*.

There had been a shipyard at Woolwich since 1485 but it had originally only been used for repair work. This was the first warship to be built at what would become the Woolwich dockyard, and the largest of its kind to be launched in the country at that time. It is perhaps surprising that she was built at Woolwich, as it was one of the smaller naval dockyards. As late as 1584, wage bills indicated that the yard was very much in fourth place:

Chatham	£3,680
Deptford	£205
Portsmouth	£30
Woolwich	£18

The ship was variously described as 1,000 or 1,500 tons, a new measurement introduced in the Middle Ages, and originally 'tuns'. The disparity might be explained by differences in measurement. Tonnage was originally a measure based on the number of tuns or barrels of wine a vessel could carry. She obviously did not carry that many barrels of wine, but she was designed to have 43 heavy bronze guns with 141 light guns and had a full ship's complement of up to 700 men. But tonnage came to have different meanings, and the vessel could have

Henri Grace à Dieu, built for Henry VIII as depicted in the Anthony Roll of Henry VIII's Navy (1545).

been estimated as its overall weight when fitted out with armament or without its heavy fittings. The hull was carvel built, and it was estimated as being 190 feet long, 50 feet maximum beam with a draught of 20 feet. The forecastle in the bow was four decks high, and provided accommodation for the men, and also carried a long bowsprit. In warfare it still acted as a fighting castle, being used by the archers who would have been included in the crew. The hull had a tumble-home design, that is it was wider nearer the waterline than at the level of the top deck. This allowed extra space on the gun deck, which was equipped with portholes for a mixture of brass muzzle loading cannon and iron breech loading guns. She was later modified and reduced in size, with a smaller crew in fewer guns.

Her wreck was discovered in the Hamble in the 1930s, and investigation revealed that the hull was constructed of three layers of planking, with the inner planking narrower than the other two. All the seams were arranged so that the overlapping planks met in such a way that the top three overlaid the next two below them, the inner planks covering them all. In effect, the seams were well covered, and the hull had a thickness of five planks. Unfortunately, the timbers have not been preserved.

This was a formidable warship, and saw action during the Battle of the Solent, fought against a French invading armada in 1545. The attempted French invasion was successfully repulsed but in the battle another of Henry's great ships sank. The *Mary Rose* was slightly smaller than the *Henry* but both vessels had a common characteristic – they were top heavy. The general view of what happened on that summer day in 1545 was that the *Mary Rose*, in attempting to turn, heeled over allowing water to pour in through the open gun ports, sending her to the bottom. The remains of the hull were brought to the surface again in October 1982 together with a huge variety of artefacts. So, although all we have of the *Henry* are illustrations, a visit to the magnificent Mary Rose Museum in Portsmouth gives us a good idea of what the Woolwich built ship would have been like – and also reveals that, although she was built in Portsmouth, there are London connections.

Almost the whole of the starboard side of the *Mary Rose* had been recovered from the Solent and is now on display after years of treatment to preserve the timbers, so we have a unique opportunity to see for ourselves exactly how a ship of Henry VIII's navy was constructed and the materials that were used. The main material used was oak, and even before construction started, shipwrights would have earmarked trees for felling, some chosen because they were straight and suitable for sawing into planks, others because they were suitable for use for curved sections, such as ribs and knees. The oak is particularly suited for the latter, which are known as compass timbers. The branches of the tree tend to spread at right angles to the trunk, which makes it possible to cut a knee with the grain running true. An eighteenth-century naval almanac illustrated how different curved members could be cut from appropriate trees (below). Ships of this period required vast quantities of timber. The *Great Michael* built in Scotland in 1506 was described as having 'wasted all the woods in Fife which timbers waste wood'. The experts working on the *Mary Rose* estimated that oaks from 36 acres of woodland (14.5 hectares) would have been felled for her construction and the *Henry* being larger would have used even more.

An eighteenth century illustration showing how compass timbers of varying kinds could be cut from trees.

Once the timber had been ordered, the master shipwright would set to work designing the hull, which would involve creating accurate shapes for each of the different ribs. He would have worked using large compasses – hence compass timber. Once the design was complete, thin wooden templates, known as moulds, would have to be created and these would be used to ensure that the timber was cut to the correct curvature. The timber would be shaped using an adze, rather like a long-handled axe, except that the blade was at right angles to the shaft. At each swing of the adze, a curve would be cut in the timber. Planking was simpler and simply required sawing into straight lengths. This was done at the saw pit. Two men were required, working with a double-handled saw. The top sawyer stood above the plank and had the harder task of pulling the saw up through the wood. The bottom sawyer's task was simpler – pulling the blade back down, but he had to work in a constant shower of sawdust.

Construction, as with the vessels described earlier, would have begun by laying down the keel, which in the *Mary Rose* was in three sections, joined by scarfs. This was constructed of elm, fore and aft, with oak in the middle. After that the keelson, a timber above the keel, stem and sternposts would have been added. The sternpost was straight and vertical, which allowed the rudder to be attached. This was a massive timber that reached all the way up to top deck level, where the tiller was connected. The tiller was round in cross section, but the end was squared off to fit into a square hole cut into the top of the rudder, where it was pinned into place. The floor timbers would then have been added, attached to the keel by treenails. After that, the ribs that define the shape of the hull were installed, and beams added to support the deck planking and to give greater strength to the hull. These were fastened to the ribs by knees – 'hanging knees' below the beams, 'rising knees' above them. Once the whole frame was complete, work could continue

A Tudor shipwright laying out the lines for a ship using a large pair of compasses from Matthew Baker's *Fragments of Ancient Shipwrighting*.

on planking the hull. There is an obvious problem here. It is easy enough to fasten planks together in straight lines, but ships' hulls are curved, so the planks would need to be bent. This was achieved by steaming the wood, when it becomes flexible. It then had to be put in place very rapidly and clamped ready to be permanently fixed in place, Once the hull was complete it was still necessary to keep the seams watertight by caulking, filling the gaps with oakum made from old rope ends. This was forced into the gap by a special caulking tool with a triangular blade. After that, the seam was covered by tar. Fixtures such as cabins would be added later. Methods scarcely changed over the centuries during which wooden ships were built. The men in the photograph (below) are holding tools that would have been familiar in Tudor times, adzes and caulking hammers.

We have no written records of shipbuilding before 1586, when Matthew Baker, son of a master shipwright from Henry VIII's reign, produced his *Fragments of Ancient Shipwrights*. In general, shipwrights kept their methods closely guarded secrets, known as 'mysteries', and in the dockyard the word of the master shipwright was law. Perhaps too much was made of these mysteries,

Building a wooden vessel at a yard in Porthmadog in 1900. The tools they are using would have been familiar to a Tudor shipwright; the man on the left holds a caulking hammer and the man next to him an adze.

for as late as 1852, the author of the *Nautical Mirror* wrote rather scathingly of the nature of early shipbuilding:

> Science has comparatively little to do with the matter. A few general principles, no doubt, gave a basis, but the superstructure was greatly an affair of guess-work and eye-work. Frames were laid down from 5 to 10 feet apart, near the centre of the vessel. Others were then placed at a distance of 20 feet or so, from the bow and stern; and all the rest of the work was done at the arbitrary pleasure of the builder, by his individual caprice or conjecture.

That may well be true, but those who worked on the preservation of the *Mary Rose* told me how impressed they were with the quality of the workmanship.

Among the many artefacts that were brought to the surface from the *Mary Rose* were a variety of guns of different styles and sizes. The most impressive were

Another illustration from Matthew Baker's book. This one shows the 'tumblehome' shape of the hull and the man up the ladder is carrying a knee that will be used to join a beam to the side of the hull.

the bronze cannons, one of which had the makers' name cast in the following inscription: ROBERT AND JOHN OWYN BRETHERYN BORNE IN THE CYTE OF LONDON THE SONNES OF AN INGLISSH MADE THYS BASTARD ANNO DNI 1537. A bastard was simply a type of gun, and others had such blood-curdling names as 'murderer' and 'grete murderer'. Casting in bronze dates back to a time before guns were introduced, when it was used for making bells. One of the earliest bells for which we have a known maker is the bell in Westminster Abbey, which has the inscription 'Christe Audi Nos' cast into it, and was made by Richard de Wymbels, who had a foundry in London between 1280 and 1320. By the fifteenth century, London had several bell makers in an area round Aldgate. Casting bells required great precision if they were to sound well, so the bell founders were the ideal people to turn to when it came to casting ornate guns. There is a popular myth that Henry VIII ordered the bells of London to be melted down to provide bronze for his fleet's cannon, which is untrue – bell bronze is a different alloy from gunmetal bronze. The story probably arose simply because he turned to the bellmakers for the manufacture. The Owyn brothers were almost certainly not the only ones making bronze guns for Henry in London.

Casting involved first making a mould of the gun with all its decorative details in place, together with a central core. The space between the mould and the core was then carefully filled with molten gunmetal. Analysis of the bronze from the *Mary Rose* showed it to be one part tin to twenty parts copper. Once the mould was full, the metal was allowed to cool slowly before the mould was broken open. The mould could not be reused, so no two guns were ever quite the same. When completed, the guns were mounted on wheeled carriages, and the explosive charge would be added down the mouth of the gun, rammed home and finally the iron ball would be dropped in place ready for firing.

Most of the guns on the *Mary Rose* and the *Henry Grace á Dieu* were made of iron. Some were cast, but this was not very satisfactory. Cast iron is brittle, strong in compression but weak in tension, and therefore always liable to fracture when fired. The majority of the guns were therefore made of wrought iron, which has exactly the opposite characteristics to those of cast iron, being flexible and strong in tension. The name 'gun barrel' that is still in use gives a clue to how they were made. Strips of

Ship's guns from the wreck of the Tudor warship *Mary Rose* in the Mary Rose Museum: the one nearest the camera is iron, the other cast in bronze.

iron, like the staves of a wooden barrel, were set in place over a central core, and then iron hoops were heated to red hot, and forced over the strips. The hoops shrank on cooling, binding the strips tightly together. A variety of different guns were found, from swivel mounted to hand held. Unlike the cannon, they were breech loaded, so that the guns did not have to be moved back after each firing for reloading. The guns were not the only weaponry recovered; 139 yew longbows and 3,500 arrows were also recovered from the wreck. The guns for the *Henry* were stored at the House of Ordnance at Woolwich, the starting point for the Woolwich Arsenal.

Other recovered items give an indication of how the ship was worked, and something of the life on board. One discovery was part of what was then a comparatively new invention – the ship's log. This was a wooden float that was attached to a cord, which had knots at regular intervals. The log would be thrown overboard, where it would remain more or less stationary as the ship sailed on. On board, a sailor would upend an hour glass and count the number of knots that passed through his fingers as the distance between the ship and the log increased. The number of the knots that passed until the sands in the glass ran out would give the speed of the ship – which is why ship speeds are still measured in knots and results entered in a log book.

Some of the things discovered certainly came as a surprise to me when I was shown them. Why did a warship have lots and lots of bricks on board? The answer was to be found in the ship's galley on the bottom deck. They were used to form safe enclosures for the fires that would be lit to heat two giant copper cauldrons in which the crew's food would be cooked. Artefacts were sometimes pleasing, at other times alarming. A full set of musical instruments was found and several different games, all of which helped to pass the time when not engaged in the serious business of battle. A giant hypodermic syringe, however, suggested that one only visited the ship's surgeon if it was absolutely essential. There was a pleasing, if slightly macabre discovery, in the carpenter's workshop. It seems he had brought his dog with him, as its skeleton was recovered – though whether it was there as a pet or to keep the holds clear of rats we will never know.

Among the other wooden items recovered were blocks, basically parts of pulley systems for controlling the rigging, and rigging was an essential part of the whole ship building process. It can be divided between standing rigging, such as the stays used to stabilise the masts and the ratlines, up which the sailors clambered to reach the higher sails, and the running rigging, used to control the movement of spars. All this involved immense quantity of rope, which was manufactured in rope walks. In Tudor times, all rope would have been made of hemp. The first stage of the process was to align the fibres and remove any tangles, by hackling, running the fibres through a set of iron spikes, set close together. The fibres could now be used to make yarn. At one end of the rope walk there was a wheel, usually about three foot in diameter, containing four regularly spaced hooks. The spinner had the hackled hemp wrapped round his waist, and at the start of the process he drew out some fibres, twisted them between finger and thumb and attached them to one of the hooks and repeated the process with the other hooks. He then began to walk slowly backwards as his assistant, usually a young boy, began turning the wheel at a steady rate, twisting the hemp strands together. At the end of the long walk, the boy detached the end from the hooks and fastened it to a winding reel. Now the spinner walked forward as the completed yarn was wound on. The process was

repeated until the reel was full, with around 250 pounds of spun yarn. A similar process is then used, with the spun yarn replacing the hackled hemp, to create ropes and ropes, in turn, could be twisted to make cable.

One of the earliest London rope works of which we have a record was the Royal Ropeyard at Woolwich, built in the 1570s, but there were certainly other rope works along the Thames before that. Street names are a giveaway – within easy reach of the river you can find Ropemaker Road, Ropemaker's Fields, Ropemaker Street, Ropewalk Gardens and more. The actual rope making process was mechanised at the end of the

Rope making by hand in the eighteenth century. The man is pulling out the hemp fibres from the bag round his waist, while the boy is turning the wheel to twist them together.

eighteenth century, but we'll take a leap forward in time to describe the process here. Although no rope works have survived from the period in London itself, there is a splendid example at the former Royal Naval dockyard at Chatham that is still in use today, and the original machinery was made by the London company of Maudsley Sons and Field in 1811.

The building itself is a quarter of a mile long which would have enabled them to produce cable that would allow a ship to drop its anchor to a depth of forty fathoms, which would require 120 fathoms (240 yards) of cable. The process started with the raw material that would have already been turned into twine by workers in a neighbouring building. The individual lengths of twine were fed into a mechanism at the far end of the ropewalk. They were then passed through holes in a metal plate to separate them, and then forced through a narrow tube. What emerged might look like rope, but it had no strength as the twines are not twisted together. This was

then attached to a hook on a revolving plate, mounted on a wheeled carriage, known as the forming machine. The carriage was then pulled slowly back along the ropewalk, and as it moved gearing made the plate rotate. Originally the forming machine was worked manually by a capstan, later by a steam engine and today by an electric motor. At the end of the run, the formed rope ran over a drum and was steadily pulled off to lie on the floor. The process could be repeated with the first strands being united until rope of the appropriate thickness had been obtained. There was one other additional process at the naval dockyards, the addition of the 'rogue's thread', a length of coloured yarn running right through the rope. Each of the naval yards had its own identifying colour, so that any rope that was being sold outside the yard that contained the thread had to have been stolen. Some of the machinery in use at Chatham has been replaced over the years but one of the original forming machines is still in regular use there.

The rope works at Chatham Docks. The machine in the photograph is one of the originals built by Henry Maudsley and still in use today.

Much of the rope was used for rigging controlled by blocks, hundreds of them for a single ship, and in Tudor times they would have been made by specialist craftsmen. They could be quite complex, with curved outer shells and a pulley made of a suitable hard wood such as lignum vitae in the centre. As with rope making, mechanisation would eventually take over from the old craft. The first big change came when Samuel Taylor developed a system for making standard sizes with machinery – at first worked by hand then, later, literally by horse power with the horse walking round a track to turn a shaft with gears to the mechanism. When a devastating fire at a naval base destroyed thousands of blocks, he was given an exclusive contract by the Navy in 1770 to make the replacements.

Marc Brunel, father of the famous Isambard Brunel, came to England as a refugee from the French Revolution, having first spent some time in America. It was during his stay in America that he first hit on the idea of revolutionising block making. In his scheme, instead of having a craftsman make a complete block from start to finish, he would have a whole series of machines, each one of which would make just one part of the block or perform a single function. Shortly after arriving in England, he met Henry Maudsley, the engineer who had founded Maudsley, Sons and Field who made the machinery for the Chatham rope works. Brunel showed Maudsley his plans and they agreed

to co-operate on producing the machines. They were fortunate in finding in Samuel Bentham, the Inspector-General for the naval dockyards, a man who, unlike many of his colleagues, was open to new ideas. Thanks to Bentham, agreement was reached in 1802 to establish a block making mill at Portsmouth using the Brunel design, with all the machines being made in London by Maudsley. Altogether, 45 separate machines were designed and manufactured and two steam engines installed to provide the power. They were divided into four categories: the first sawed the timber into appropriately sized, squared blocks; the next set were used for boring holes, shaping the block and cutting grooves; the third set produced the central pulley and the fourth made the pins to hold the pulley in place. The shaping machine was the most complex as it had to produce an accurately curved surface.

The mill was an immediate success and by 1818 was turning out around 160,000 blocks a year, sufficient to supply all the main naval bases. The mill building is still there, but most of the machinery has gone. However, one can still see one of the machines in the Portsmouth Historic Dock Museum and admire the ingenuity of Brunel and the engineering skill of the London manufacturer. It represents one of the earliest examples of mass production technology. The only people who were not delighted by the success were the Portsmouth block makers; where once a hundred

One of the blocks recovered from the *Mary Rose*.

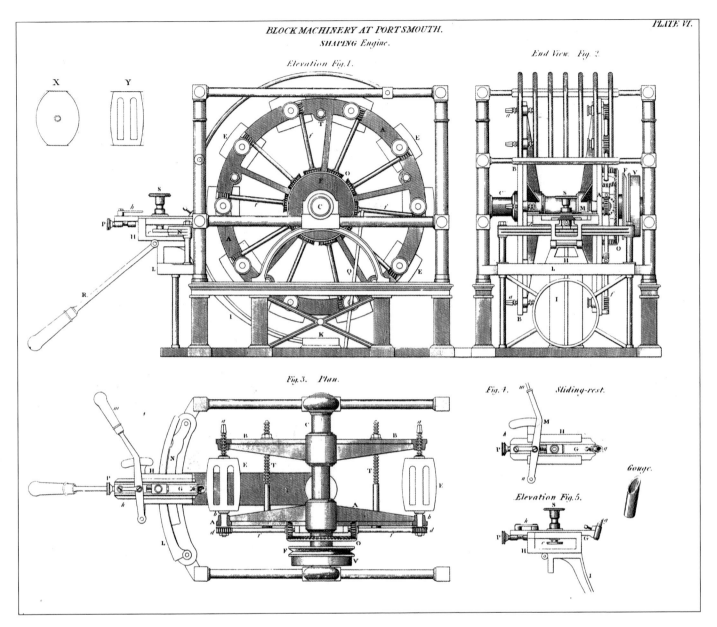

BLOCK MACHINERY AT PORTSMOUTH.
SHAPING Engine.
Elevation Fig.1.
End View. Fig.2.
PLATE VI.
Fig.3. Plan.
Fig.4. Sliding-rest.
Gouge.
Elevation Fig.5.

One of the machines designed by Marc Brunel for making blocks. The previous illustration shows how smoothly the main body is curved, and this machine was used for shaping.

had been employed, now only ten were needed. Marc Brunel also developed mechanical saws, establishing his own sawmill at Battersea and arranging for a mill to be established at Woolwich Arsenal.

Sails were among the last items to be added to a ship. Sail making may seem straightforward, simply get a lot of strong cloth, such as canvas, stitch it together and the job's done. It is not that simple. The sail loft needs to be large for obvious reasons. Sails not only come in different shapes and sizes, but the cloth has to be cut so that it has a 'belly' – in other words if it is laid on the floor and all the edges pulled out, it will not lie flat. Calculating the correct draft to make an appropriate amount of belly is an important part of the sail maker's craft. The sewing requires very strong thread and a sturdy needle – the sail maker will need a leather palm to protect his hand. The edges of the sail are sewn to create hems, and then reinforced with rope. A number of eyelets have to be made for fastening the sail to the spar and for passing through the ropes that will control movement. Tabs are attached to the sail so that it can be reefed, rolled up to shorten it and fastened securely

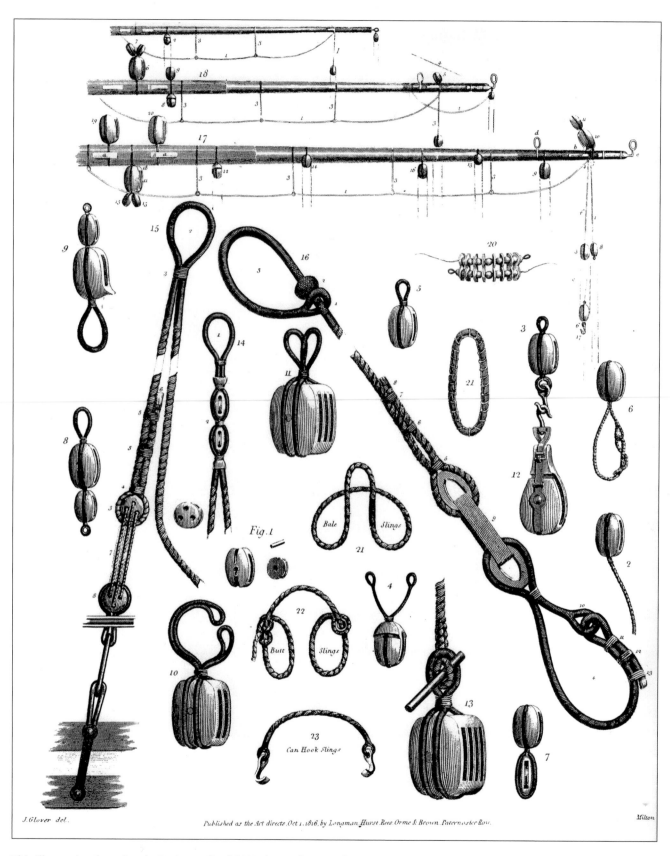

J. Glover del.

Published as the Act directs, Oct 1.1816, by Longman, Hurst, Rees, Orme & Brown, Paternoster Row.

Milton.

This illustration from Rees's *Cyclopaedia* of 1819 shows the complexity of rigging for a large ship, including standing rigging on the left and running rigging at the top, used to control the movement of sails and spars.

if the wind becomes too strong. The tabs are, of course, fastened by reef knots, secure but easy to untie. This is a gross simplification that would probably make an experienced sail maker wince, but hopefully it gives some idea of the complexity of the craft.

We have been looking – with a few diversions – at ship building in the reign of Henry VIII in some detail to give an idea of the complexities of ship construction in the age of sail. Now it is time to move on to see how shipbuilding developed over the next few centuries. One major change that was to make ship design far more accurate was introduced by Matthew Baker, the son of Henry VIII's master shipwright, James Baker. He devised a system for showing the different cross sections of a hull by drawing on paper. An example, showing the details of an eighteenth-century man of war, can be seen on the right. Each curved line is numbered to indicate which part of the hull it refers to. Baker was immensely influential, and his successor Phineas Pett wrote to him in 1603, 'although I served no years in your service yet I must ever acknowledge what ever I have of any art (if I have any) it came only from you'. Pett, however, turned out not to have all that much art after all: his first ship was declared 'altogether imperfect'. However, he went on to build better vessels, and also to be something of a rogue, using Admiralty material to build private vessels for his own profit. He survived for a long time but was eventually dismissed and his son took over.

The royal dockyards at Deptford and Woolwich were expanded over the years. They were busy places, teeming with many kinds of activities. Carts and barges would be arriving bringing timber. The amount needed by any one ship was measured in loads, a somewhat vague term that simply meant the amount of wood that could be carried in a cart drawn by a single horse. John Smeaton, the eminent civil engineer, carried out experiments in the eighteenth century and recorded that $5/8$ of a ton was the average that could be managed on a soft road – and before the eighteenth century virtually all roads were soft. We do not have figures for many early ships, but we do know that when Nelson's ship, the 64-gun *Agamemnon*, was built, it required 2,000 loads. That was a lot of timber to be delivered and a lot to saw and shape.

The royal dockyards on the Thames finally closed in 1869 and although they were making steam ships towards the end, they were all constructed with wooden hulls. The last sailing vessel to be built by either yard was the 50-gun *Nankin* in 1851. However, there were other major shipyards along the Thames throughout the age of sail. They were all, of necessity, built downstream of the old London Bridge – the narrow arches made it impassable by large craft. Above the bridge, only smaller vessels, such as barges and lighters, could be built. Rather than go through them all, and there were dozens of them, we shall be concentrating on the most important, the Blackwall yard. Anyone wanting a comprehensive list should try and get hold of a copy of Philip Banbury's *Shipbuilders of the Thames and Medway* (1971).

The yard was first laid out in the 1580s, but its early prosperity was to be based on building vessels for the Honourable East India Company. That trading organisation was first formed in 1599 and awarded a Royal Charter by Elizabeth I that gave them a monopoly on all trade east of the Cape of Good Hope for 15 years. The name 'Honourable' was not always appropriate, as from the 1620s they were heavily engaged in the slave trade and remained in that infamous business until it was abolished by law in 1807. But in the early years, most of their trade was with India. As their name suggests, that was not what they had hoped to be doing. They originally intended to grab a part of the lucrative spice trade from the East Indies, but the Dutch had beaten them to it, so India was very much a second choice. They initially began building ships for the trade at a yard in Deptford but soon outgrew that and moved to a better site at Blackwall. There is some doubt as to whether the Company ever actually owned the yard, but their presence was vital to its success, and the Company's motto was inscribed on a ship's bell in the yard and their coat of arms was set into a tablet. The first ship recorded as built under this regime was the Indiaman *Globe*. This would have been a typically broad beamed and heavily armed vessel, looking very like the naval vessels of that time. She needed the armaments as the Indian Ocean was notorious for its pirates and privateers. In time, the East India Company began to charter ships rather than have them constructed, but Blackwall continued to build typical vessels for the eastern trade, and it seems produced more of them than any other yard.

In 1655, the yard was sold to Henry Johnson, later Sir Henry, who had begun his working life as an

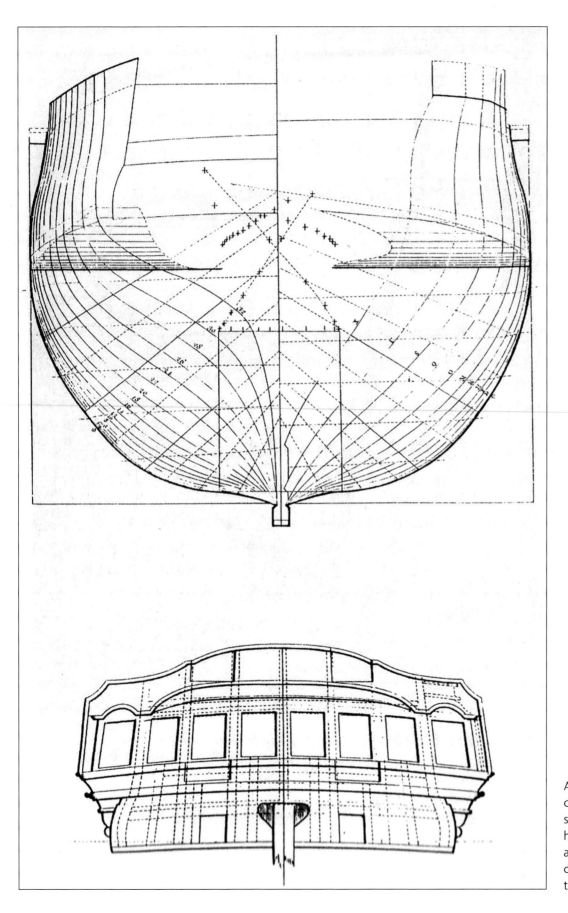

A master shipwright's drawing c.1800 that shows the shape of the hull at various points along its length and the details of the stern where the captain had his cabin.

This painting of an East Indiaman in the Thames by William Adolphus Knell (1801-75) shows a storm damaged ship returning to the docks for repair.

apprentice to his uncle, Phineas Pett. At that time, the yard contained three docks, two launching slips and storehouses, all contained within a high wall. During the Commonwealth years, Johnson was responsible for building battleships for the navy, but with the restoration of the monarchy, he immediately set out to demonstrate that, rather like the Vicar of Bray, he would serve whoever was in charge. As a mark of allegiance, his first ship after the Restoration, an Indiaman, was named *Royal Oak*. One member of the Navy Board was the famous diarist Samuel Pepys. And though his diaries have a fund of information about life in London at that time, there is not a great deal about the docks. He did, however, make a special mention of visiting Blackwall and of ships built

there that were designed by Sir Anthony Deane. In his entry for 19 May 1666, he wrote:

> Mr. Deane and I did discourse about his ship *Rupert* built by him there which succeeds so well as he hath got great honour by it, and I some by recommending him; the King, Duke, and everybody, saying it is the best ship that was ever built.

Pepys also recorded that Blackwall had 'the largest wet dock in England' and belonged to the East India Company. When Johnson was knighted, he had his house in the dockyard rebuilt in a grander style as befitted his new status.

Ships on the Thames at Rotherhithe by Thomas Whitcombe (c.1763-1824). A number of merchantmen are under construction at the shipyard.

After his time, the yard passed to the Perry family, who continued their lucrative connection with the East India Company; the records show that of 31 large ships built between 1756 and 1767, 27 were Indiamen. One reason the numbers were so large was that the ships were only expected to make four round trips before being laid up, each voyage lasting around two years. The main problem that caused the short working life was the damage caused to wooden hulls by various kind of marine life, including barnacles and the ship worm, *Teredo navalis*. In 1708, Charles Perry suggested that the problem could be solved by attaching a thin layer of copper sheeting to the bottom of the vessel. The ever-conservative Admiralty turned the idea down. It was another half century before the idea was given a full trial and proved a success in 1761. Over time, it became accepted as essential for wooden

vessels intended for long voyages. So successful was the scheme that the phrase 'copper bottomed' came to be used for any venture offering a sound return to investor.

The yard grew and developed over the years. In 1789, the Brunswick dock was built with two basins – the larger able to hold thirty Indiamen. The most prominent building that can be seen in the illustration on page 33 is the tall mast house. The typical main mast of an Indiaman was over a hundred foot long and weighed around nine tons. Being able to store such masts below made it far easier to crane them out and lower them into the hull. Over the next few years, the yard changed hands several times and continued building sailing ships right into the 1840s. Ship construction developed only slowly. One major change was the replacement of the tiller on large vessels by the wheel. The lateen sails

Brunswick Dock by William Daniell (1769-1837). The tall building is the mast house, where masts could be stored vertically, ready to be craned into place.

were seldom seen but were replaced by triangular sails set as staysails between the masts and on the bowsprit, and often with a fore and aft sail on the mizzen, known as a jigger or spanker. But, in general, cargo vessels were still slow broad beamed craft. A real change came in the 1830s.

Blackwall had found a new and lucrative trade in the Far East that was demanding fast vessels. They began building opium clippers. 1839 had seen the start of the first of the Opium Wars between Britain and China that forced the Chinese to deal in the drug against their will. It was one of the most discreditable episodes in the building of the British Empire in the holy name of free trade. The clippers were the ultimate in fast sailing ships, and although no London built clipper has survived, one famous ship is on permanent display at Greenwich, the *Cutty Sark*. The first clippers were designed in America, where the hunt for speed began during the war of 1812,

when they began building privateers. After the war, they turned to two lucrative trades where speed was of the essence – slave trafficking and opium. The ship that epitomised the early clippers was the *Ann McKim* built in Baltimore in 1832. She was square-rigged on three masts, long and shapely, with a length to beam ration of 5 to 1 and she had the most distinctive feature of all clippers, steeply raked and hollow bows. It is a measure of just how successful the American clippers were that Blackwall were building their clippers just seven years later. The clippers continued to be built, but with a less noxious trade in mind – bringing tea from China. This is the trade for which the *Cutty Sark* was commissioned to be built on the Clyde in 1869, but which she was never destined to serve. That was the year the Suez Canal was opened, enabling steamers to reach China – and the clipper sailed instead to Australia to collect wool. She remained working under sail right

The famous tea clipper *Cutty Sark* at her permanent berth at Greenwich.

through to the 1920s, when she was bought by Captain Wilfred Downman for just £3,750 and was restored and brought to her final home for display. We can assume that the Blackwall vessels may have had a very similar appearance.

Even before the first clipper was built, however, the yard had also turned to a new form of construction. In 1821, the *City of Edinburgh* was launched, not a sailing ship but a steamer. The London shipyards were entering a new era.

CHAPTER 3

RIVER TRAFFIC

The Thames is not merely the river that runs through the heart of London; for centuries, it was the main thoroughfare. Until the late eighteenth century, there was only one bridge across the tidal river, the old London Bridge that was first built in 1176 and which remained as the only bridge on the tideway until 1729 when the first Putney Bridge was completed. London Bridge was constantly jammed with traffic on the narrow roadway. If in Elizabeth I's reign you wanted to see the new play that Mr. Shakespeare was putting on at The Globe and you lived north of the river, then the easiest way to get there would have been by boat. But the bridge was not only inadequate for coping with road traffic, it was also a problem for any boat wishing to pass through its narrow arches. For large craft, as mentioned in the previous chapter, it was an impenetrable barrier and for smaller vessels a serious hazard. On the ebb tide, it acted as a dam and it was estimated that the difference between the levels on either side was a staggering five feet or more, and the water poured through with a roar that could be heard far inland. For those who had to make the passage it was like shooting the rapids. One traveller wrote of 'water piled up to a much greater height than we in our little ship' and many capsized and lost their lives.

Old Putney Bridge from Walter Armstrong's book *The Thames*. This rather flimsy looking wooden bridge was the first to be built across the river since the medieval London Bridge was constructed.

As a result of this congestion, there was a rich variety of vessels on the river. There were small boats to carry passengers, across and up and down the river – in effect water taxis. Then there were the lighters that took cargo between the larger ships and the various wharfs and the barges that carried goods into and out of the capital. As well as the small passenger boats for hire, there were several ferries crossing the river. Looking at illustrations from the period, it seems a miracle that there were not endless collisions, with boats moving in

The Pool of London crowded with ships below London Bridge.

all directions – up and down and across the river. We shall start with the small craft and the watermen who worked them. John Stow in his *Survey of London* of 1603 described the Thames as having '2,000 wherries and other small craft' and E. W. Brayley, writing in 1796, gave an even greater figure of 3,419 small craft.

There were two classes of boat in regular use, the wherries, large rowing boats with six or eight oars, and the scullers or oars, worked by just one man. The watermen who had a monopoly of the trade, would wait by the various stairs, the old equivalent of a taxi rank, and shout out 'Oars, oars'. There is a story of a French visitor who mistook the call and was disappointed when he found he had paid sixpence for a river trip and not for a visit to a lady of pleasure. Looking through Samuel Pepys' Diary from 1659 to 1669, one is struck by just how often he was using the river to get about, sometimes

finding the river crowded with boats. On 2 November 1660, he wrote: 'to White Hall, where I saw the boats coming very thick to Lambeth, and all the stairs to be full of people. I was told the Queen was a-coming, so I got a sculler for sixpence to carry me thither and back again.' But he never did get to see the Queen. It was not only the living who used the river. The previous month he had seen the body of the Duke of Gloucester being carried down the stairs at Somerset House to be taken by boat to Westminster for burial. His most dramatic account of river traffic appears in September 1666 when he was witness to the great Fire of London. In this part of the description, he had just received news of the fire:

So I down to the water-side, and there got a boat, and through bridge, and there saw a lamentable fire. Poor Michell's house, [which was on London Bridge] as far

The Stairs at Queenhithe from Armstrong's book on the Thames. The Stairs were places along the river where boatmen collected passengers.

as the Old Swan, already burned that way, and the fire running further, that in a very little time, it got as far as the Steele-yard, while I was there. Every body endeavouring to remove their goods, and flinging into the river, or bringing them into lighters that lay off; poor people staying in their houses as long as till the very fire touched them, and then running into boats, or clambering from one pair of stairs by the water-side to another.

The watermen did not always enjoy the best of reputations and a number of Acts were passed with the idea of improving the services they supplied. The first came in the reign of Henry VIII in 1514 that required watermen to work for sixpence a day and only to charge authorised fares. But in 1555 another Act was scathing in its comments on the way the system worked.

Whereas heretofore for Lack of good Government and due Order amongst Wherrimen and Watermen exercising, using and occupying Rowing upon the River of Thames, there have Divers and many Misfortunes and Mischances hapned and chanced of late Years past, and a great Number of the King and Queen's Subjects. By Reason of the rude, ignorant and unskilful Number of Watermen, which for the most part being masterless Men and single Men of all Kinds of Occupations and Faculties, which do work at their own Hands, and many Boys being of small Age, and of little Skill, and being Persons out of the Rule and Obedience of any honest Master and Governor, and do for the most part of their Time use Dycing and Carding, and other unlawful Games, to the great and evil Example of other such like, and against the Commonwealth of this Realm.

The Act also reported that 'divers Persons have been robbed, and spoiled of their goods, and also drowned'. To remedy the situation, the Act authorised the appointment of eight Overseers to monitor the river between Windsor and Gravesend. It also insisted on a one-year apprenticeship, later extended to seven years. That seemed not to have worked, for by 1700 the watermen were being described as 'more numerous and disorderly than before'. Now all the different watermen were brought under the control of the 'Watermen's, Wherrymen's and Lightermen's Company'. The rules laid down that all these men must be registered with Trinity House. We think of Trinity House these days as simply being in control of lighthouses, but it was originally set up in 1514, following a petition from Deptford seamen, complaining about the lack of control of pilots working on the Thames. Henry VIII awarded a charter to what was then known by the elaborate name: 'the Master, Wardens, and Assistants of the Guild or Brotherhood of the most glorious and undivided Trinity and of St. Clement in the Parish of Deptford-Strood in the County of Kent'. One can see why it was abbreviated to Trinity House. Their first role was to regulate pilotage and it was only in the reign of Elizabeth I that they were given the added responsibility to be in

Boatmen on the river were controlled by Trinity House. The organisation also provided alms houses for the elderly, and this fine model of an Indiaman graces the building.

charge of sea marks, the role they still fulfil today. With the 1555 Act, their activities were extended to control all the watermen on the river, and they set out a series of rules and conditions.

Anyone found to be working who was not registered by Trinity House could be fined £5 for every week they worked. As they would be highly unlikely to afford such fines – with a purchasing power of around £600 today – they would probably have ended up in a debtors' prison. An abstract of the new rules was published in 1708. A waterman could, for example, take as many apprentices as he liked, but no apprentice could take charge of a boat 'till he hath Rowed two Years with an able Waterman'. There were rules about plying for hire, which were intended to prevent the arguments that all too regularly broke out by making it a punishable offence to try and coax away 'any Person about to take Water with another'. Passengers were supposed to be protected from pestering by crowds of watermen touting for custom at the various approved stairs. Judging by the Rowlandson cartoon of a scene at Wapping, this does not seem to have worked very well (below).

The rules for watermen decreed that they should never hustle customers, but if this drawing by Rowlandson of 1812 is anything to go by, the rules were definitely ignored.

Lightermen had their own set of rules, one of which was intended to prevent the accidents that had occurred when going through the arches of London Bridge. Only one lighter at a time was allowed through at high tide and anyone who passed through on the flood and then got themselves grounded were fined five shillings. The authorities were well aware of several sharp practices and set out rules to try to either prevent them or, if that failed, punish anyone found out. For example, anyone buying coal from a collier from the north east and then trying to pass it off as coal of a higher quality was to give forty shillings to the poor. It seems that the lightermen were not only known to try and cheat the general public but were not above trying to nobble the competition. 'He that loosens another's Lighter from his proper Foot, shall make good the Dammage sustain'd and forfeit 5s and make Satisfaction to the Party wrong'd'.

Certain standards of behaviour were expected. They were not allowed to work on Sundays unless they had received special permission from the authorities and they were forbidden to swear in front of passengers and, which seems very reasonable, they were not allowed to work when drunk. However, a pamphlet *A Kind Caution to Watermen* written at the time suggests that, in respect to language at least, the rules were none too strictly applied. When the author travelled by boat he heard 'men bellowing out their lewd and filthy jests, treating one another with all the opprobrious language their Wit can invent and in pretence of being in jest all the while, uttering those things, that are not fair to be nam'd among Christians.'

There were many happy to criticise the men who worked the Thames, but few to support them. Probably few of the watermen themselves were literate and even fewer had the time or inclination to put pen to paper. One exception was John Taylor, known as 'the waterman poet'. He was born in Gloucester in 1580, but moved to London, where he served as an apprentice waterman and became an enthusiastic supporter of his occupation. He wrote a book, entirely in verse, *The Description of the Two Famous Rivers of Thame and Isis* in 1632, in which he described the Thames from Oxford to London. At that time, the river above and through Oxford was the Isis and only when it was joined by the River Thame did it become Taylor's Thame-Isis or Thames. On the upper reaches, he was constantly annoyed by the weirs, built by millers to enable them to divert water to work their machinery. Sometimes, weirs crossed the whole river, and the only way boats could cope with these was by flash locks, in

A flash lock on the Thames. The lock keeper is lifting the vertical pieces, the rimers, which will allow the water through, and will then move the top timber to open the gate and allow the boat to ride down on the flood or flash of water.

which sections of the weir were composed of a wooden structure that could be removed, a section at a time, to let a flash of water through. Boats could ride the flash down or be winched up against the flow. It was a hazardous business and in 1634, a passenger boat with sixty aboard capsized in the Marlow flash, with no survivors. The following is a typical comment by Taylor.

Haules Weare doth almost crosse the river all,
Making the passage straight and very small.
How can that man be counted a good liver
That for his private use will stop a river?

He was acutely aware of the criticisms he and his fellow watermen endured and when he arrived in London, he had a new source of complaint – too many citizens were using land carriages instead of travelling by water.

For though the King, the Councell, and such States
As are of high Superior rankes, and rates,
For port or pleasure, may their Coaches have,
Yet tis not fit that every Whore or Knave,
And fulsome Madam and new scurvy Squires,
Should jolt the streets in pompe, at their desires:
Like great triumphant Tamberlaines, each day,
Drawn with the pamper'd Jades of Belgia.
That almost all the streets are choak'd outright,
Where man can hardly passe from morne till night.
Whilst Watermen want worke, and are at ease
To carie one another, if they please,
Or else sit still, and poorly starve and die,
For all their livings on foure Wheeles doe fly.

The Tower of London by Wenceslaus Holler. It shows the variety of craft to be seen on the river in the seventeenth century, including two lighters at anchor and a variety of passenger boats.

Taylor was not alone in worrying about the problems facing watermen. Petitions and counter-petitions flowed into parliament, not always being quite what they seemed, as Pepys discovered on one of his trips by boat in February 1659:

> In our way we talked with our waterman, White, who told us how the watermen had lately been abused by some that had a desire to get in to be watermen to the State, and had lately presented an address of nine or ten thousand hands to stand by this Parliament, when it was only told them that it was a petition against Hackney coaches: and that to-day they had put out another to misdeceive the world and to clear themselves.

In a prose work, *The Arrant Thief*, Taylor defended the honour of his profession:

A waterman cannot be false to his trade for he has no weights or measures to falsify, nor can he curtail a man's passage: his worst fault is, that like a lawyer he will take more than his fee … his bare fee he will take willingly (upon necessity) but less than his fare, or many times nothing, me thinks goes against the stomach.

The fares seem reasonable. In the list of prices in the 1708 rules, for example, the fare from London Bridge to Limehouse is listed as twopence a sculler, and a trip all the way from the centre of London to Windsor was fourteen shillings for a single passenger, with other passengers paying just two shillings each. When I was reading the documents in the Bodleian Library in Oxford, I found a hand-written note of the period giving the carriage fare from Haymarket to Red Lion Square as one shilling and sixpence.

Three winners of Doggett's Coat and Badge, from 1900 and 1901, while the splendidly bearded gentleman in the centre won the event in 1850.

One other of Taylor's complaints was that theatres were being built on the north side of the Thames, so that most Londoners did not need boats to visit them. One theatre man did, however, acknowledge the work done by the watermen. Thomas Doggett, who had been the manager of Drury Lane, died in 1721 and in his will, he left a sum of money to provide a Coat and Badge as a prize for a race to be run annually for young watermen between London Bridge and Chelsea. The boats were the usual passenger boats in which they worked the rest of the year and they had to row the 4 miles 5 furlongs against the ebbing tide. The race is still run annually as it has been for the last three centuries, making it the oldest race on the river. The better-known Oxford and Cambridge Boat Race is a comparative newcomer that was first held in 1829.

The work of the lightermen was needed because of the nature of the river until the nineteenth century. The most

obvious difference was the complete absence of enclosed docks in which water levels could be maintained at any state of the tide. As a result, vessels drawn up against a quay would literally be left high and dry at low tide. This presented a real danger for larger craft that were in danger of keeling over. As a result, they had to anchor, mainly in the section of the river between Limehouse and London Bridge – the Pool of London. Smaller coastal vessels would be nearest the banks, larger vessels near the centre of the Pool. The biggest ships, the Indiamen, rarely travelled higher than Blackwell. Frank G. C. Carr in his book *Sailing Barges* (1931) quotes a writer called Stockwell describing the scene in 1796:

A stranger would naturally look for the quays and wharves made for the accommodation of this great quantity of shipping; but he would learn, that except the *legal* quays about a quarter of a mile in length

The Oxford and Cambridge boat race of 1841, an engraving from an original by Francis William Topham (1808-77).

between London Bridge and the Tower, the rest of the business is done at the sufferance wharves, irregularly interspersed on the banks, and so inadequate to the purpose, that lighters are obliged to be employed for the loading and unloading of a great proportion of the goods, to the heavy expense and detriment of the merchant. He would also lament the contraction and embarrassment of the stream from the tiers of ships moored in the midst of it, and reaching from each side, so as at some times scarcely to afford a passage, and liable to various injuries.

The legal quays were the places where the majority of goods could be landed according to legislation first passed in Tudor times. The sufferance quays were places where certain bulk goods could be landed, such as coal. The lighters would work with the tides as far as possible, using sweeps to steer, moving upstream on the rising tide and travelling down on the ebb. They were also rowed. Lighters continued to be used in this way well into the twentieth century.

One major event that brought river traffic to a halt was the great freeze of 1563. With the Thames frozen solid, people could walk from one bank to another. The boatmen, however, were quick to take advantage of the situation and set up booths at the steps to charge people the usual fare for the crossing. No one objected, for the river became the scene for a great Frost Fair,

A crowded scene near Limehouse by Thomas Serres (1759-1820), with a lighter loaded with hay, a small boat being sculled and a narrow boat being loaded by the quay.

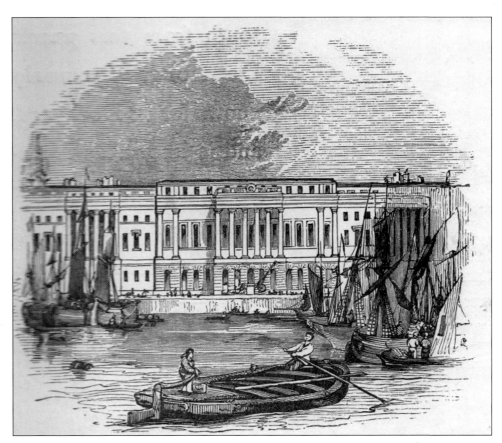

Right: A lighter being worked with a sweep, a long oar, near Somerset House: an illustration from Armstrong's Thames book.

Below: An early twentieth century photograph of lighters lined up at Limehouse; it is notable that these appear to be all commercial buildings with their own landing stages – one building has a sign announcing it is the premises of a mast and block maker.

with stalls selling goods, an ox roast on the ice and entertainments of all kinds were laid on. There were other times when the river froze over the succeeding years and yet more Frost Fairs were held.

The Thames was not the only river in which the watermen plied their trade. They also worked the rivers and creeks that fed into the main river, notably the Lea and the Fleet. The latter was dredged in 1502 'so that boats with fish and fewel were rowed to Fleete Bridge and to Oldbourne Bridge, as they of old time had been accustomed, which was a great commodity to all the inhabitants of that part of the city'. This happy state of affairs did not last long as the river became little better than an open sewer. The playwright Ben Jonson described its condition in his *Epigrammes* of 1616 and what awaited anyone trying to row through its waters:

Which, when their oares did once stirre,
Belch'd forth an ayre, as hot as the muster
Of all your night-tubs, when the carts doe cluster,
Who shall discharge first his merd-urinous load.

A century later and, if anything, things had got even worse and it was not only the merd-urinous filth that was being tipped into the Fleet as the eighteenth century *Tatler* described in doggerel:

Sweepings from butches' stalls, dung, guts, and blood,
Drown'd puppies, shaking sprats, all drenched in mud,
Dead cats and turnip tops, come tumbling down the
    flood.

After the Great Fire, Sir Christopher Wren produced plans for reconstructing the area that included covering

The Frost Fair of 1814 by Luke Clenell (1781-1840). When the river froze the boatmen made up for their loss of income by charging visitors to the fair.

The entrance to the River Fleet can be seen under the high-arched bridge in this painting by Samuel Scott (1702-72). At this time the river was still navigable.

over the Fleet. The plans were rejected, but in 1680 the river was canalised to improve navigation. However, it was little used and in 1737 part was finally covered to create the Fleet Market, and the process of covering the whole of the Fleet was completed in the 1860s. Today it is one of London's lost rivers, remembered only by the name Fleet Street.

Ferry services were quite different from the other forms of river transport. Like the watermen, they carried passengers, but some also carried horses and carriages – and even, in the rural areas to the west of the city, cattle. They operated a regular service between two landing stages facing each other across the river. The rights for running such services were valuable and much cherished.

In the absence of bridges, ferry services appeared at regular intervals all down the tideway. There is a wealth of information on these ferries in Joan Tucker's *Ferries of the Lower Thames* (2010) which I have used as my main reference for most of the following. Joan was a friend, who died recently, but I am sure she would not have objected to my making such liberal use of her work – using the signed copy she gave me.

It would not be appropriate here to give details of every single ferry; instead, I have chosen a few that have interesting histories as representative of so many more. The journey starts at the western end of the tideway at Twickenham, where more than one ferry operated over the years. The rights to operate a ferry usually rested with the largest landowner, in this case the Earls of Dysart of Ham House. The earliest reference shows a ferry operating in 1659 but could well have been in use earlier. The first record to provide significant details is a lease to run the ferry awarded to William Blower in 1692 at an annual rent of forty shillings. He died in 1694, but his widow continued to operate until she died in 1704. The lease now passed to Thomas Love and when he died his widow again carried on with the business until her death in 1744; obviously ferrymen's wives were quite formidable ladies.

This was a profitable business and inevitably others tried to set up a rival service. Two men, Treherne and Langley, opened a ferry service close to the official one, but were promptly taken to court where they were charged sixpence as a penalty and sixpence costs – not exactly a huge sum but a deterrent, suggesting that

The horse ferry at Isleworth by Joshua Cristall (1767-1847). It is typical of many ferries in the London area.

any further attempts might receive harsher treatment. However, Margaret Langley, widow of the original offender, with a partner, Samuel Kain, gave Earl Dysart a £100 bond, having said she was operating 'a publick ferry' but she would not interfere with the original. There were further attempts over the years to set up rival ferry services.

By the middle of the nineteenth century, Twickenham and Petersham were developing as prosperous, middle class residential areas. However, there was growing concern about the loss of attractive green spaces within easy reach of London as more and more land was disappearing beneath suburban villas. In 1895, the National Trust was set up to preserve ancient buildings and to protect the countryside. They campaigned for guaranteed public access to the Thames, and the Richmond, Petersham and Ham Open Spaces Act was passed, ensuring the survival of a large open space on the Surrey side of the river. At the same time, the London County Council acquired the Marble Hill estate on the opposite bank. There was a problem, however, for would-be visitors. Getting to these spaces from Richmond Bridge was difficult, and the Dysart Ferry landed passengers a rather uncomfortably long way from the areas. Nevertheless, the ferry did a roaring

trade. In 1891, William Champion, who had worked on the Dysart estate, was appointed ferryman and he and his wife moved into the newly built Ferry Cottage. Mrs Champion rented a property for £1 a week next to the ferry landing place on the Surrey side, where she sold refreshments. The business thrived and Champion soon had three boats, each able to carry up to twenty passengers, and was employing a 'strong boy' to help him.

It was inevitable that once again a rival would appear on the scene. This time it was a licensed waterman, Walter Hammerton. He reached an agreement in 1908 with the Council to moor a floating boathouse near Marble Hill, from which he rented out skiffs and punts. Rather conveniently, there were steps across the river from the boathouse and anyone arriving on the opposite bank wanting to hire a boat could wave across and Hammerton or his partner would row across to collect them. He would also be prepared to fetch others, who just wanted to cross the river, for a fee. He might have managed to continue uninterrupted, but the passenger business was proving increasingly lucrative, and he painted the word 'Ferry' on the boathouse. He was now in direct opposition to the Dysart interests, and the whole matter finished up in court. It turned out to

The ferry at Twickenham from an old postcard. The owners had a profitable business running a tearoom at the landing stage.

be a protracted battle. At the first hearing, Hammerton won the right to operate his ferry, but then the Dysart-Champion interest went to the Court of Appeal, where the judgement was reversed. This time it was Hammerton who took the last step – he took his case to the House of Lords, where he won. It was a costly affair, and as both ferries continued to operate at a profit, could have been settled if the two sides had not been so obstinate. The situation was not helped by bad personal relations between Champion and Hammerton.

The Dysart family left Ham House and presented it to the National Trust in 1948, and with the change the running of Twickenham Ferry passed to a private operator. Revenue steadily declined and it closed in the 1970s. The Hammerton Ferry, however, is still operating. There was, however, another ferry service in the area taking people to Eel Pie Island. There had been an inn on the island from 1743 and later what had been a rather grand gentleman's residence was transformed into a hotel. It became famous as a music venue – home

to fashionable dance bands in the 1920s, traditional jazz in the 1950s and several rock bands who later went on to play somewhat larger venues, including the Rolling Stones, The Who and Pink Floyd. It was later to fall into disrepair and burned down in 1961.

This has been the story of just one small area, on the outskirts of London, served by ferries, but it perhaps illustrates that this was a vital service to the community and a potential source of a good income to operators. There were regular ferry crossing points all the way down the Thames, many of which had fascinating histories. One of these was the Lambeth Horse Ferry. It is not difficult to locate where it once ran, as Horseferry Road still exists and leads straight down to Lambeth Bridge. It connected two of the capital's most impressive buildings, the Palace of Westminster and Lambeth Palace, home to the Archbishop of Canterbury. It was the most important ferry in the City of London area, as the only one authorised to carry horses. References go back as far as

Most of the Thames ferries have gone, but Hammerton's ferry from the village of Ham is still running after over a century in operation.

the thirteenth century, when there was a dispute over the fees paid, between Lambeth and St. Peter's Abbey in Westminster. The crossing was not always easy. In 1633, the ferry was carrying Archbishop Laud with his servants and horses, when it sank. All managed to escape, but the Archbishop's life was literally cut short in 1645 when he was beheaded. Oliver Cromwell suffered a capsize as well in 1656 and though he escaped, the horses drowned. One of the most dramatic events came in 1688. In November of that year, William

of Orange landed in England, with the intention of taking over the throne from James II. The latter made only a feeble attempt to prevent it happening, and as William advanced to London, James's Queen Consort, Mary of Modena, decided to escape to France, taking her baby son with her, also nursemaids and two trusted aides, St. Victor and the Count de Lauzun, were in the party. St. Victor later wrote an account of the events, which opened with the group making their way to the Lambeth ferry, 'our passage was rendered very difficult and dangerous by the violence of the wind and heavy incessant rain'. They made it safely, but there was no coach waiting, and the Queen and her baby had to huddle down beside Lambeth Old Church, while St. Victor went to fetch the carriage. Eventually, they made it to Gravesend and set sail for France, where she was to remain as the 'Queen over the water' for the rest of her life. In later years, the ferry interest were strong opponents of all attempts at getting permission to build a bridge at Lambeth. But eventually, the bridge was approved in 1756 and the Archbishop was paid £3,780 as compensation for loss of revenue. But as the bridge seems to have been used exclusively by vehicles, the ferry continued to operate until a suspension bridge was built in 1862, itself to be replaced in the twentieth century by the present bridge.

As the number of bridges across the river grew, so more and more ferry services came to an end. One that has survived since Norman times is at Woolwich. The first ferries were serving a rural community, but with the development of the Royal Arsenal, more and more traffic appeared and the Army began their own ferry service in 1810. This was closely followed by a private company, which collapsed in 1844. In 1846, the Eastern Counties and Thames Junction Railway decided to take over. They built a branch line down to the river and instead of the old craft brought in three paddle steamers. By 1880, the service was considered to be hopelessly inadequate and a new, bold idea was put forward. The Metropolitan Board of Works had taken on responsibility for London's bridges and abolished tolls. As the ferries were supplying the same service, taking Londoners from one side of the river to the other, why should that not be free as well? To the delight – and probably surprise of the locals – the idea was adopted and the free ferry service still runs.

In their day, the watermen of London through their wherries and ferries provided the city with essential services, equivalent to those supplied by the buses and tube trains of today. But there was also another form of water transport that played an important role – the barges that carried goods into and out of the capital. The early barges were very simple in design, little more

Lambeth horse ferry and Lambeth Palace by Jan Griffier (1652-1718). The ferry was operated by a chain – the ferry man can be seen winding the handle to move the vessel along. It is a little surprising to see nude bathers in the centre of London,

Above: The Woolwich steam ferry: this has always been run as a public service free of charge.

Below: The paddle steamer *Gordon* at the Woolwich pier.

than straight sided, flat bottomed wooden boxes, but with sloping ends, rather like overgrown punts. There was a single mast set forward, which could be lowered for going under bridges by a simple windlass. A tiny cabin had space for two to sleep. The sail could only be used when there was a favourable wind. The illustration below shows several barges of this type – those heading down stream have the wind in their sails, but those heading on the opposite direction are being hauled along from the towpath. Here horses are being used, but often the work of towing upstream went to gangs of anything up to eighty men to haul a barge that might have 70 tons of cargo on board. The men who skippered the barges heading up towards Oxford and beyond were known as the western bargemen, and as well as cargo, they were often happy to take passengers on board as well. One Londoner who enjoyed their company was Samuel Pepys, who often refers to them in his diary. For example, on 14 May 1669, he wrote:

> So home, sullen: but then my wife and I by water, with my brother, as high as Fulham, talking and singing,

and playing the rogue with the western bargemen, about the women of Woolwich, which mads them, and so back home to supper and to bed.

We never discover what the story of the Woolwich women was – though he reports telling it to another western bargeman – but it was probably scurrilous.

Over the years, the hulls of these simple craft were given slightly more rounded and graceful lines, but they were still a very long way from being the craft we think of as Thames barges today. Their most distinctive feature is the spritsail, which appears to have first been developed by the Dutch. The sail is still square, but instead of being set at right angles to the mast, as in the earlier barges, it is aligned fore and aft. The forward edge is attached to the mast, and the sail is extended by means of a spar – the sprit – that runs diagonally from the foot of the mast to the top corner of the sail, the peak. The lower end of the sail can be controlled by a rope known as the sheet, while the top of the sprit is steadied by a pair of ropes, reaching down to either side of the deck, the vangs (pronounced 'wangs'). The bottom

Barges working above London Bridge were known as Western barges. In this view of the River at Windsor in the middle of the seventeenth century, typical box-like sailing barges can be seen coming downstream, while a team of horses haul another barge past a mill stream.

of the sprit rests on a rope collar round the bottom of the mast, the snotter. When the sail is not in use, it is brailed, pulled in towards the mast. The spritsail barges were developed so that they could be used for short sea voyages round the south east coast, but there a new problem arose. The barges were mainly flat bottomed, where sea-going vessels would have a keel to prevent them skittering across the water. The answer was to use lee boards. These were two heavy, wooden boards, one on each side of the vessel and, as the name suggests, one would be lowered into the water on the lee side to do the same job as a keel, while the one on the far side remained raised. When a barge is tacking, at each change of direction, the crewman would take the sheet from one side to the other, raise the lee board that was in the water and lower the one on the opposite side. Having crewed Thames barges myself, I can testify that winching up the lee board is definitely hard work. Over the years, there were further developments in barge design, but before looking at those developments, this is an appropriate time to look at the life of the barge men in the early years.

Accidents were far from unknown, and if there was a fatality, then it was a double blow to the owner.

The Thames sailing barge *Carthusus* in the Thames estuary; a larger barge with sails on the bowsprit can be seen in the distance.

Due to a curious law known as a 'deodand' anything that caused a death was forfeit to the crown – and if someone drowned in a boating accident then the boat was said to be the instrument of death and could be seized. It does not always seem to have been enforced, but amazingly it remained law until 1846. One of the greatest calamities occurred during the great storm that hit London in November 1703 and records show that over 1,000 chimneys were blown down, church roofs were ripped open and there was havoc on the river. All but four of the ships in the Pool lost their moorings and were driven ashore; wherries were sunk and some sixty barges were driven by the wind to pile up against the piers of London Bridge. There was another great gale in 1768, but the losses were not as great. But one can imagine the scene in the darkness of night with a howling wind, and the bargemen and sailors desperately trying to save their craft from destruction – and in some cases losing their lives in the attempt. They had good reason to be desperate, for a bargeman who lost his vessel, lost his livelihood. Those were days long before marine insurance became commonplace. Collisions on the crowded river were by no means unknown and when one looks at the statistics for 1796, one can see why. The list of small vessels on the Thames included 85,103 barges and 15,454 lighters. Add to that list other even smaller vessels and the grand total came out at 110,156. Then there were the ships at anchor in the pool, and between dodging each other and trying to avoid the moorings of ships, it is a surprise that any vessels made progress without hitting something.

The barge men had a reputation for not always being the most honest of citizens, which given the fact that their pay was for many years governed by law and was scarcely enough on which to keep a family, is not altogether surprising. The barges were perfect for smuggling. They could go out to meet vessels and take off taxable goods, which would have otherwise been noted by the customs officials when the vessels reached port. There was a good chance that, as barges were not known for making trips across the Channel, they would escape inspection. One type of vessel was particularly well suited – the hay barge, also known as a stackie, a very appropriate name since when fully loaded it looked like a floating haystack. Away from the river, traffic of coaches and carts all depended on horses, who needed to be fed. The barges brought in the hay, stacked as high as twelve feet on the deck – and ideal for hiding contraband somewhere in the middle. Nevertheless, some were caught and in 1828 a Revenue Cutter captured the barge *Alfred* with 1,010 half-ankers of contraband spirit – that's around 5,000 gallons. The hay could be brought quite long distances and the record was held by the barge man who was master of the *Farmer's Boy* from Suffolk. In a single year he brought in 52 loads from Harwich to Vauxhall, returning with loads of manure for the fields. Given that he must often have encountered bad weather, especially in winter, he must have worked virtually non-stop. Such barge men may have been smugglers on the side, but most simply worked hard all their lives.

Over the years, the Thames barges developed and their rigging became more complex. A topsail was added above the main sail and a short mizzen was set in the stern. The larger vessels had bowsprits with jibs. The hull developed and became less boxy, with finer lines and they generally had more comfortable cabins, though still basically operated with just a two-man crew. The bowsprit barges are said to be the largest vessel ever to be worked by such a small crew. In later years, the wooden hulls gave way to ones of iron or steel. Some of the biggest changes came as a result of the annual barge matches inaugurated in 1863 by Henry Dodd. He started his working life as a ploughboy, but went on to start a highly lucrative business, tendering barges to carry the city's waste away to be dumped in the countryside. He was convinced that the competition would encourage boat builders to make improvements in order to win the prizes, while at the same time demonstrate the seamanship of the barge captains. There were two classes taking part: topsail barges up to 100 tons burthen, and 'stumpies', up to 80 tons but without topsails. The prizes for the winners were an £18 cup to the owner and £10 10s for the crew, with lesser amounts for second and third. Similar prizes, but slightly less in value, went to the stumpies. By the time the second race came round, there were forty barges competing. Dodd died in 1886 but left £5,000 in his will to ensure the annual races continued. They did and do continue, but now the barges no longer carry cargo, but have been converted for pleasure use. That, however, does not diminish the magnificent sight of these wonderful vessels under sail.

Eighteenth century revenue officers on the Thames dockside.

A sailing barge being loaded with hay.

A hay barge under way in central London; the tall structure is a shot tower, used during the manufacture of lead shot. The site is now occupied by the Royal Festival Hall.

The fifth annual barge match of 1867 with *Renown* in the lead, from a print by John Taylor.

I have been fortunate enough to crew in a few matches over the years – never, alas, in a winning boat. But although everyone wants to win, these are by far the most exhilarating events in which I have ever been involved. Some owners employ retired barge skippers to take charge on match days and talking to the professionals gives an insight into their way of life, their skills and their toughness. One of these gentlemen had tried to remain in business, long after most had retired for lack of cargos. The only way he could do it was by working single-handed. It is difficult even to try and think what that entailed, having to be at the helm and work all the tackle on his own. One can only stand and admire.

Although sailing barge traffic was greatly diminished at the start of the Second World War, the vessels were to take their part in the extraordinary flotilla of small ships that set out to rescue the British troops from the beaches of Dunkirk. Altogether sixteen barges took part and many failed to return: some that were damaged were simply beached and abandoned. One of these, however, the *Ena*, in Frank Carr's words 'took such a strong dislike to her position that she sailed herself home, alone and without a soul on board, and was later found empty and comparatively undamaged on Sandwich Flats'. One barge that did return was *Pudge,* now restored and owned by the Thames Sailing Barge Trust. The barges were especially valuable. They could be towed across the channel and then with their shallow draught they were able to get in close to shore, but that of course put them in the greatest danger. A former barge hand, F. S. Fullar, who had been called up for service, witnessed them arriving:

I was profoundly impressed by the string of sailing barges go past in tow, bound for the hot spot I had just left. Realising the courage needed to man such a craft on such an errand, they made, to me, an unforgettable picture. At the wheel of each barge stood the skipper, as imperturbable and solid as those I had served under, apparently unmoved by the somewhat fearsome danger awaiting in and above those waters.

Where the great majority of barges were purely functional trading vessels, some were specially built for important occasions. Among the great ceremonials of London, the Lord Mayor's Day annual procession has been a major event for many centuries and for most of that time it took place on the water. The Lord Mayor's barges have always been elaborate affairs, with teams of rowers and sumptuous gilded decoration. On the day, he would have been joined by other similarly gaudy vessels, belonging to the various livery companies. The earliest reference dates back to 1422 when the Brewer's Company recorded 'That Sir William Walderne was chosen Mayor on St. Edmunds Day, when it was ordered that the Aldermen and Craft should go to Westminster with him to take his charge, in barges without minstrels'. By the sixteenth century, the day was formalised. The procession would be led by the Mayor's barge, followed by that of his own liveried company, followed by the barges of the eleven remaining companies in order or precedence, with the Mercers at the top of the list and the Clothworkers bringing up the rear. There would have been masques and pageants on the day, organised by the Mayor's company. If the royal barge also took part, then it was given precedence, and all the other barges would line up along the bank to allow it to take the lead, and then fall in behind.

Royal processions along the Thames became quite common with the Tudors. When Anne Boleyn was crowned queen, she was described as wearing rich cloth of gold and was accompanied by musicians for the journey down the river. It was not to be very long before she was to make another journey down the Thames by barge, this time without any rich garments or musicians, but to the Tower for her execution. Queen Elizabeth I was very fond of river processions, and whenever she set forth, she did so in style, often accompanied by mayoral and company barges. These were grand occasions and Shakespeare's famous lines from Antony and Cleopatra were surely more apt as a description of the Queen of England's progress than that of the Queen of Egypt.

The barge she sat in, like a burnish'd throne,
Burn'd on the water; the poop was beaten gold,
Purple the sails, and so perfumed, that
The winds were love-sick with them, the oars were
    silver,
Which to the tune of flutes kept stroke, and made
The water which they beat to follow faster,
As amorous of their strokes. For her own person,
It beggar'd all description; she did lie
In her pavilion, - cloth-of-gold of tissue …

An anonymous painting of the Lord Mayor of London's procession in front of Westminster Palace in 1683. He is accompanied by the equally ornate barges of the different Liveried Companies.

We get a hint of what these royal processions were like in Stuart time from Pepys, who watched one in 1662, when as well as the barges there were two pageants presented on the water 'one of a King and another of a Queen, with her Maydes of Honour sitting at her feet very prettily'. There would have been music on these occasions, but we have little idea of what any of it would have been like until the eighteenth century, when George I made a journey from Whitehall Palace to Chelsea on 17 July 1717, a date possibly chosen for its palindromic quality – 17.7.17 – and commissioned music for the occasion from Handel. This became the famous suite, known as Handel's *Water Music*, and on this occasion it was played by an orchestra of fifty musicians travelling in a separate barge. The king was so impressed that when he disembarked at Chelsea, he ordered the musicians to stay behind and had the whole piece repeated on the return journey.

River pageantry suffered a severe setback in the middle of the nineteenth century, when river pollution became an ever-increasing problem. Untreated sewage and other unsavoury matter was being dumped in the Thames, a problem that was ignored until the river became so foul that it produced what came to be known as 'the great stink'. No one wanted to travel by water unless they had to – and certainly royalty and the Lord Mayor had no wish to suffer the horrors. The 'stink' actually did Londoners a favour. The city was regularly suffering from outbreaks of cholera and at the time no one knew that contaminated water was the cause. Various proposals were made for dealing with the problem but were ignored by parliament. But the stench of 1858 could not be ignored. The new House of Commons was right by the river and although attempts were made to hide the smell by hanging curtains soaked in vinegar in the building, it was intolerable. As *The Times* noted, 'proximity to the source of the stench concentrated their attention on its causes in a way that many years of argument and campaigning has failed to do.' It was the engineer Joseph Bazalgette who came up with the solution. He designed a new sewer system that was to run along both banks of the river to a pumping station

George III and Handel on the occasion when the king was entertained on his voyage by musicians in the accompanying boat. The music they were listening to is now known as Handel's *Water Music*.

downstream, where it could be treated and released into the estuary. The sewers themselves were covered over, creating the present Thames Embankment, changing the nature of the river in this part of London, which, in effect, was partially canalised.

The royal bargemasters who had been important members of the court were no longer required. Their splendid uniforms, which since the eighteenth century had consisted of a scarlet jacket with the royal insignia, knee breeches, white silk stockings and a cocked hat, were redundant. However, to mark Elizabeth II's Diamond Jubilee in 2012, a new royal rowing barge was commissioned, based on traditional designs and as ornate as predecessors and named *Gloriana*. The splendour of river pageantry had returned. Amongst all this splendour, however, there was to be another parade in 2017, not of royal or mayoral barges, but to honour the old trading barges in a special parade from the Isle of Dogs, and Tower Bridge was raised to pass them through. It was an honour well deserved by a class of vessel that had served London well.

There were more craft on the Thames in London in the eighteenth century than there have been at any

Part of a procession of ten Thames Barges passing under Tower Bridge in September 2017.

time since. There are many reasons. First, the number of bridges crossing the Thames steadily increases from the end of the century. Even below London Bridge, where the biggest ships waited, there were new opportunities for passengers. Marc Brunel was the engineer responsible for the first tunnel under the river and, thanks to the development of hydraulics, Tower Bridge was built as a bascule that could be raised to let even the tallest ship pass through. The introduction of powered vessels brought in a new age of ever larger ships, capable of carrying far more cargo than the old sailing ships, so fewer vessels were needed. The days of sail did not end immediately, but it gradually diminished. While it lasted, the Thames in London offered a splendid spectacle, with boats of all kinds and sizes plying their trade.

A busy scene on the Thames at Westminster in the eighteenth century in a painting described as in the style of Samuel Scott.

CHAPTER 4

THE CANAL AGE

The story really begins with improvements to Britain's rivers. The big change came with the introduction of the pound lock – now simply known as a lock. In essential, the idea was quite simple. In the same way that a mill stream is created, construct a weir, and run an artificial channel from above it, to rejoin the river below the weir. Within this artificial cutting, create a watertight chamber large enough to hold the type of boat using the river, and close off both ends with moveable gates. Then create openings, either in the lock gates, or via culverts in the side of the lock and cover these with paddles that could be shifted, allowing water to flow into the lock to fill it or out to empty it. So, for a boat going downstream, the lock would be filled by raising one set of paddles to allow the boat in, and once inside, the first paddles would be closed and the second set would be raised to empty the lock, until water had reached the lower level, when the bottom gates could be opened and the boat could carry on its way. It was far safer than the old flash locks, much as walking downstairs is safer than sliding down the bannister.

Because most river navigations were worked by wide-beamed barges, the gates had to be massive as well. This created a problem – a single conventional gate that swings open would be very cumbersome but replacing that by two gates to meet in the middle only introduced another problem. Water pressure would tend to force them apart. As a result, the earliest locks had gates that were lifted vertically, which required construction of a frame and winding gear. The solution to making a system using conventional gates seems obvious now, but it took an Italian genius to come up with it. In 1492, Leonardo da Vinci was appointed ducal engineer for Milan, and one of his jobs was to design a set of locks for the *Naviglio Interno*. His sketch books show his plans for masonry locks, with gates that were set at an angle, so that they formed a triangle pointing up stream. Now water pressure, instead of forcing them apart, pushed them closer together. Because the way they met was like a mitre joint in carpentry, they became known as mitre gates. The first lock with mitre gates on a British river was built on the Lea in the sixteenth century. It was such a novelty that it even made its way into a poem of 1577, *Tale of the Two Swannes*. While not exactly a great work of literature, it does at least provide an accurate description of the lock.

> …. The locke
> Through which the boates of Ware doe passe with
>   malt.
> This locke contains two double doores of wood,
> Within the same a cesterne all of Plancke.
> Which onely fils when boates come there to passe
> By opening of these mightie doors.

This became the standard arrangement for river development over the next centuries. Details changed;

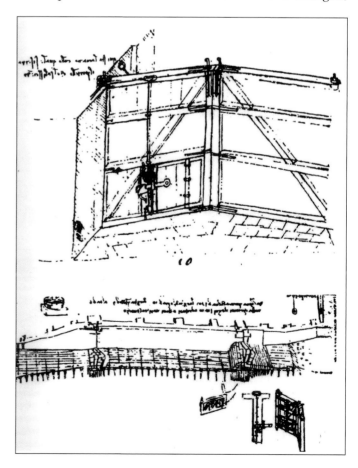

Leonardo da Vinci's sketch for mitred lock gates for a canal – a system that remains in use to the present day.

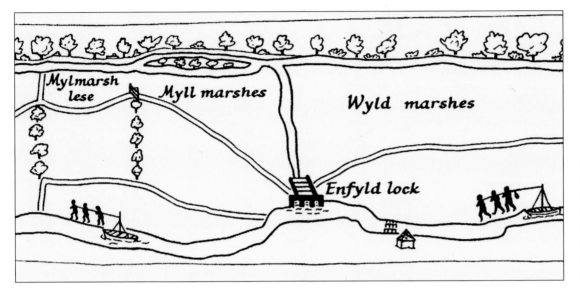

A rough representation on the River Lea in the sixteenth century, when a pound lock was constructed with mitre gates: the first on any river navigation in Britain.

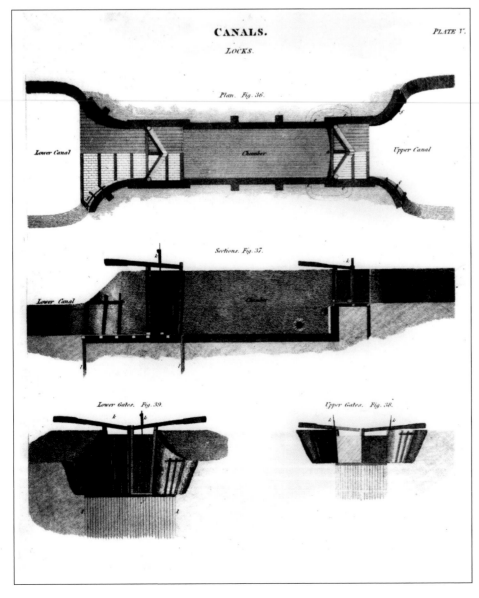

The typical layout of a canal lock from an eighteenth-century encyclopaedia.

most locks were constructed from stone rather than timber and in later years, wooden lock gates were replaced by iron or steel. Yet when the Lea Navigation was modernised in the middle of the twentieth century, the new locks would have seemed perfectly normal if Leonardo could have returned to see them. And as can be seen from the photograph on p.66, the technology of installing new lock gates would probably have been equally familiar to any time traveller.

As part of the river improvement, an Act was approved in 1766 for a short artificial cutting to be made from the River Lea at Bromley to the Thames at Limehouse. At first, when it opened in 1770, it was only wide enough to take one barge, which meant there were real problems, so a passing place was built halfway along. By 1777, it was recognised that even that was not enough to ease congestion, so the cut was widened, but not for the last time. As traffic grew, it was increased to 55ft wide and then, eventually, in the nineteenth century, to 75ft. Now it became a truly viable waterway.

There was, however, a limit to river improvement and by the middle of the eighteenth century, when Britain was about to enter a period of extensive industrialisation, there were still large areas of the country that had to depend entirely on land transport and that could be dire. The agriculturist Arthur Young spent a lot of time touring the country, comparing farming practices. In 1769, he wrote this description of the Wigan turnpike,

The locks on the River Lea Navigation were completely rebuilt in the twentieth century to allow modern, motorised barges to use them.

New lock gates being installed on a canal using shear legs, a system that would have been used when the canal was first built.

London's first canal was the Limehouse Cut that joined the River Lea at Bromley to the Thames at Limehouse and was opened in 1770. Originally only wide enough for one barge at a time to use it, it was widened at a later date, as seen here.

and readers should bear in mind that turnpikes were supposed to be the country's finest roads, which is why travellers had to pay tolls to use them. So, if this was the best the country had to offer, what must the worst have been like?

Let me most seriously caution all travellers, who may accidentally purpose to travel this terrible country, to avoid it as they would the devil; for a thousand to one but they break their necks or their limbs by overthrows or breaking downs. They will here meet with rutts I actually measured four feet deep, and floating with mud only from a wet summer, what therefore must it be after a winter?

The situation was bad, and the new industrialists were not satisfied. One of them decided to do something about it, but he was different from most of his fellow industrialists, being an aristocrat with extensive estates. It just happened that his property included coal mines at Worsley near Manchester. He was Francis Egerton, Duke of Bridgewater. He had, like other young aristocrats, gone on the Grand Tour of Europe, but while he was unimpressed by ruins and statues, he was fascinated by a splendid artificial waterway, the Canal du Midi. When he returned to England, he had a very unsatisfactory love affair, that turned him against the opposite sex for ever. He devoted himself to the mines and, realising that a waterway connection to rapidly developing Manchester would be invaluable, he tried to persuade the owners of the Mersey and Irwell Navigation to allow him to build a canal to join their waterway to complete his journey to the heart of Manchester. They refused, so the Duke took a bold decision – if he couldn't join the Navigation, he would leap across it with an aqueduct. So, in 1760, the Bridgewater Canal was opened and tourists came from miles around to marvel at the sight of boats on the canal passing high above barges on the river. Others were more impressed by more mundane matters; thanks to the canal, the price of coal in Manchester was halved. Other industrialists began to start planning canals in the north of England and the Midlands.

The engineer who had worked with the Duke of Bridgewater was a millwright, James Brindley, and now he was in demand as chief engineer for many new projects, including the very important Trent and Mersey Canal. Brindley's favourite method of construction was what we call 'contour cutting', avoiding obstacles such as hills by following the natural contours to go round them. But at Harecastle Hill, just north of Stoke-on-Trent, he was faced with an obstacle he simply could not go round nor over. His only option was to go through in a tunnel. When he had planned the extension of the Bridgewater Canal down to the Mersey, he had allowed for locks that would take barges roughly 14ft wide. Now, faced with the daunting and unprecedented task of boring for over a mile and a half through the hill, he found it was all too much. He decided that instead of building one to take 14ft wide boats, he would only allow for 7ft. Given the technology of the time, it was a sensible decision. It was actually to take eleven years to build and Brindley never lived to see its completion. But

The Duke of Bridgewater, who financed the first British canal to be built independent of any natural waterway; he is pointing to the Barton aqueduct that carried the canal over the River Irwell.

it was a momentous decision. If the maximum width of boat that could go through the tunnel was 7ft, then only boats that size could travel the whole canal. So, what was the point in building locks to take bigger craft? So, locks were built to take craft approximately 70ft long by 7ft beam, and as Brindley was also the engineer for canals that would connect with the Trent and Mersey, he built those to the same dimensions. As a result, the great network of canals that began to spread throughout the Midlands was based on the narrow boats that were to dominate canal travel for two centuries and are still to be seen in the canal pleasure boats of today.

London had yet to feel the benefit of canals connecting the city to the rest of Britain and there was a lull in construction throughout the 1780s due to a fall in trade caused by the American War of Independence.

But the 1790s saw a huge increase in canal schemes, in what came to be known as the canal mania years. The most important of these new schemes was the Grand Junction Canal, which was to link the Thames at Brentford to the Oxford Canal, and from there could connect all the way up to Manchester and the newly thriving industries of the north. There was also a branch from the main line that ended at a basin on what was then a settlement on the edge of London, Paddington. It was designed to be worked by narrow boats, which, although they carried less cargo than the river barges, were still far more efficient than any form of road transport. It was estimated at the time that a narrow boat, pulled by a single horse, could carry up to thirty tons. The canal companies, like the turnpike trusts, looked to recoup their capital and make a profit

The narrow boat became the typical craft of Britain's canal system. This heavily laden boat is on the Coventry Canal, and the boatwoman is wearing her traditional costume.

for the shareholders, by charging tolls to the users. These were set out in detail in the Act of Parliament that authorised construction in 1793.

The rates charged were based on three factors: the nature of the cargo; its weight; and the distance travelled. The cheapest rate was for lime and limestone, at ¼d per ton per mile; then came a whole range of goods, ranging from pigs to pig iron at ½d and coke and coal at ¾d. As well as these standard charges, there was also a charge of ½d per ton payable to both the canal company and the City of London authorities for every ton passing between the canal and the river. It was a simple matter to tell the distances travelled as the company could issue documents showing where the boat was loaded and where it was unloaded. Measuring the weight and nature of the cargo was rather more difficult, but a system was devised for gauging all boats using the canal. One associates the name 'Bradshaw' with railways, but canals had their own Bradshaw as well, complied by Henry de Salis, Chairman of a successful canal carrying company. His description of gauging is suitably concise and clear:

Gauging, means of ascertaining by the draught of the vessel the weight of cargo on board for the purpose of taking tolls. The first gauging of canal boats is carried out at a weigh dock, where particulars of the boat's draught are taken when empty, and when fully loaded, and at intermediate points, such as at every ton of loading. The boat is loaded with weights kept for the purpose, which are lifted on and off by cranes, the result arrived at then either transferred to graduated scales fitted to the boat's sides, which can be read at any time, or the particulars of each vessel are furnished to each toll office in a book, from which on gauging the immersion of the boat can at once be ascertained.

Where the boat's particulars were kept by book, then special gauging rods were used to check how deep the vessel sat in the water, and hence find out the weight of the load. Boatmen were always looking for ways to reduce their toll payments. If the toll keeper was at one side of his boat, he'd put his weight on the other, and it was not unknown with mixed cargos, to hide those with the highest value among the less valuable.

A pair of Grand Union Canal Carrying Company narrow boats being gauged to assess the weight of cargo being carried and the tolls that would have to be paid.

The Grand Junction was a success, but trade between sea-going ships and the canal still depended on lighters and barges on the river to bring cargo up to Brentford. In 1812, a new Act was passed for the construction of the Regent's Canal, that would extend from the Paddington basin to a new basin at Limehouse. It was to have a total of twelve sets of locks, each set having two locks side by side to ease the flow of traffic. At Limehouse, there was to be a wide lock, 350ft by 60ft, allowing ships to enter from the river. It was to have, apart from the locks, two major engineering features, a 272 yard tunnel at Maida Hill and a 960 yard long tunnel at Islington. By this time, the technology of tunnel construction was well established. The first stage was the survey to establish the height of the ground at various points along the line of the tunnel. When that was completed, it was possible to create a profile of the tunnel and the ground above it. Now shafts could be sunk down to tunnel level and the navvies could get to work. Some would start at the ends working inwards, following the compass directions as laid out from the survey, while others would work out from the foot of a shaft. It was hard, physical labour. Where rock was encountered, holes had to be drilled by hand and filled with gunpowder for blasting. At Islington, tracks were laid to take simple box wagons. When these were filled with spoil, they could be taken to the foot of the shaft, where the box could be lifted from the chassis and hauled to the surface. We know this because there is a very rare illustration showing the work going on, by the light of flares (left). I began researching canal navvies over forty years ago, and this is the only illustration I have ever found from the canal age showing navvies at work.

The canals proved a boon to many haulage companies. One of the most important was begun by the Pickford family from Poynton in Cheshire who set up in business in the early eighteenth century, running trains of waggons between Manchester and London. These would have been slowly trundling, broad wheeled waggons hauled by a team of eight horses. They offered a service twice a week from both places. The arrival of canals in the north of England offered something of a challenge and they bought their first boat in the 1770s but by 1790 boating was still only a small part of a very big business, with 28 waggons, 252 horses and only 10 boats. All that changed when work started on the Grand Junction. They at once saw its potential and acquired premises at Paddington even before the canal was open for business. The company grew and prospered and the canal trade steadily increased, but the family proved to be poor managers and were soon heavily in debt to the canal company, with tolls unpaid. Most of the family simply sold their shares, leaving it to two of the younger Pickfords – Thomas II and Matthew II – to try and rescue the concern. They failed, and though the Pickford name lived on, the family were no longer involved. It was soon a thriving concern again.

They continued to run between London and Manchester, but with the opening of the Regent's Canal, they moved to a new base at City Road Basin at Islington. They prided themselves on running a uniquely fast service, using fly boats that worked

Navvies at work during the construction of Islington tunnel on the Regent's Canal. Spoil from the workings is being hauled to the surface up a construction shaft.

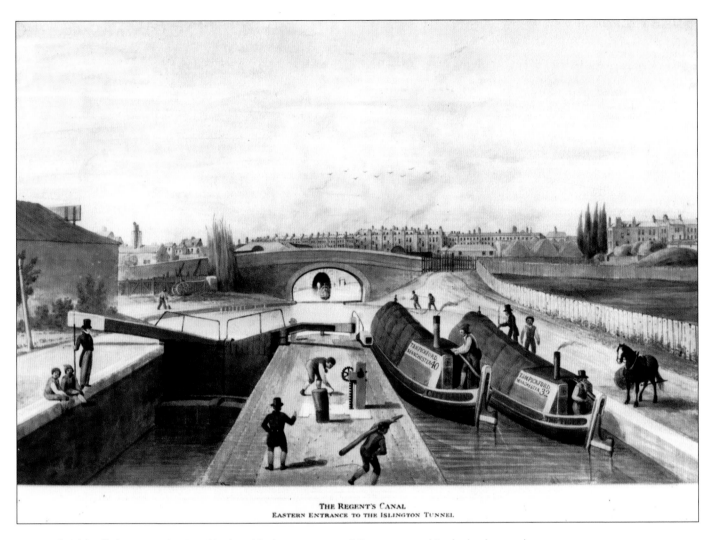

THE REGENT'S CANAL
EASTERN ENTRANCE TO THE ISLINGTON TUNNEL

A pair of Pickford's boats at City Road locks with the entrance to Islington tunnel in the background.

non-stop, day and night, to a strict timetable. This involved changing crews and horses at intervals along the way. They were officially given precedence over other craft on the waterway, though quite how that worked in practice is not altogether clear. Somehow one can't see the skipper of a rival boat, politely saying 'after you' and ushering in a Pickford boat ahead of his own. By 1820 they owned 80 boats and would eventually have 400 canal horses to work them. In August 1842, *The Penny Magazine* published an article describing the operation at City Road, which they claimed to be the largest canal operation in Britain. It is worth quoting at length as a unique insight into what the coming of the canals meant to London:

This large establishment nearly surrounds the southern extremity of the City Road Basin. From the coach-road we can see little of the premises; but on passing to a street in the rear we come to a pair of large gates opening into an area or court, and we cannot remain here many minutes without witnessing a scene of astonishing activity. From about five or six o'clock in the evening waggons are pouring in from various parts of town, laden with goods intended to be sent into the country by canal. In the morning, on the other hand, laden waggons are leaving the establishment, conveying to different parts of the metropolis goods which have arrived per canal during the night.

On entering the open area we find the eastern side bounded by stabling, where a large number of horses are kept during the intervals of business. In the centre of the area is the general warehouse, an enormous roofed building with open sides, and on the left are ranged offices and counting-houses.

To one who is permitted to visit these premises there is perhaps nothing more astonishing than to see upwards of a hundred clerks engaged in managing the business of the establishment … Let us now suppose that a London Merchant wishes to send a cargo of goods to Manchester per canal, and that is through the machinery of Messrs. Pickford's establishment that the transaction is to be effected. There are, in addition to receiving-houses in different parts of town, two offices, one at the east, and the other at the west end of London, where merchandise is collected for canal transit … One of the two town-offices, the 'Castle' in Wood-street, presents an animated and bustling scene towards evening when waggons laden with packages during the day, are about to be dispatched to City Road wharf. On arriving at the wharf, each waggon draws to by the side of an elevated platform, provided with convenience for unloading waggons and loading boats. From the southern extremity of the basin a branch turns to the east, nearly separating the yard into two portions. The portion on the southern side of this branch is called 'the dispatch charging warehouse' and that to the northern the 'shipping warehouse'. The waggons coming in laden with goods, proceed to the shipping warehouse, where they are unladen, and the goods placed temporarily in groups on the platform of the warehouse. Each group is to form the cargo for one boat, so that there are as many groups as there are cargoes. The boats are drawn up at the side of the 'shipping warehouse' and are there laden.

All this activity had to be accompanied by clerks making out invoices for the different items and making entries for the office. Yet it was possible to get half a dozen boats away in the evening that the loads arrived, with everything fully documented. It was a highly efficient operation, but the company always had its eye on increasing efficiency and raising profits. Once railways reached London, they began to cut back on canal transport and in 1847 they announced that they would cease to take anything by canal the following year. Although the City Road operation was unique, the busiest spot on the system was the great basin at Limehouse. It was the one place where cargoes could be unloaded directly from ships into narrow boats.

Limehouse Basin, where the Regent's Canal joins the Thames. The ships are being loaded and unloaded by a mixture of barges and narrow boats.

It was not only goods that were taken by canal. There was also a regular passenger service between Paddington and Uxbridge. The canal was even used by individual pleasure boats and a narrow boat permanently moored on the Regent's Canal offered small boats for hire. An account of a pleasure trip on the Regent's Canal appeared in Harper's *New Monthly Magazine* in 1885, but the anonymous author did not seem very impressed by the scenery:

Meantime we have been slowly passing, on the right, the great dreary goods station and the yards of the Great Western Railway. Then we come to Paddington work-house, a long dreary brick structure, set in a vast dreary field; and now beyond it, at the side of the Harrow Road, stands the Lock Hospital for destitute fallen women.

Passing under Harrow Road bridge, we burst into a silent sea of shabby gentility, drearier in its assumption than all that has gone before. A pretentious terrace stretches away on either hand, faced with a make-believe massive balustrade, cracked and broken; the heavy houses fronting upon it are stuccoed shams, seamed and shabby; its few disconsolate trees seem tired of trying to keep up appearances, and the faded grass is completely discouraged and is going back again.

The packet boat on the Grand Junction Canal ran between Paddington and Uxbridge. It was pulled by a pair of horses.

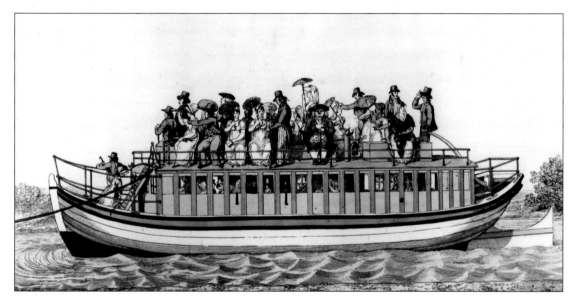

Pleasure boats were available for hire on the Regent's Canal in the early nineteenth century.

Times certainly change. It is hard to recognise this as a description of Little Venice, where one of those 'stuccoed shams' would probably set you back several million pounds.

For part of the journey they travelled by narrow boat, and if the authors took a jaundiced view of the canal, the boatman was even more damning:

It's never clean, an' it's allers low water, and there's nothin' but naked man a' bathin' and thieves wot robs your barge and takes all they can git out of 'er, and blackguard boys wot calls yer names and spits on yer, and throws stones at yer.

Travel on the Regent's Canal has certainly improved since then.

In the early days, the only means of moving the boat was a single horse and on the Regent's Canal there was one point when even that was no longer of any use. Islington tunnel was built without a towpath, which meant that the boat had to be legged through. This involved the boatmen lying on their backs, with their feet

Trip boats at Little Venice in the middle of the nineteenth century.

against the tunnel walls, and walking the boat through. It sounds arduous, but having tried it myself, I found that once the boat was under way, it was strenuous but not excessively so – and the tunnel is comparatively short at just over half a mile – legging the Standedge tunnel on the Huddersfield Canal at over three miles long would have been a very different proposition.

The boats themselves became standardised. There was a sort of foredeck in the bows, then the cratch, a vertical wooden section, from the top of which planks were laid all the way back to the rear cabin in the stern. Waterproof cloths could be draped over the top planks and fastened down to keep cargo dry. The cabin itself was roughly ten foot by seven foot and this had to be a miracle of organisation as, unlike the fly boats run by Pickford's which had an all-male crew, it was home to the whole family, boatman, wife and children. Although everything was kept to a bare minimum, there were essentials including a cooking range, a cupboard with a door that folded down to make a table and a complex arrangement of beds. In the stern was the curved wooden tiller, which could be removed from the stern post and pointed upwards to create more space when moored up for the night. Although the facilities were limited, the boat families made the best of them. Cabins were decorated by hanging colourful plates on the wall and the brasses were kept brilliantly polished and the stove black leaded.

Life for boating families was never easy; everyone who was old enough was expected to do their share. Nell Cartwright began her boating before the First World War, working from the age of eight. She was usually up at four or five in the morning, putting the kettle on the stove for tea. Her main work was looking

The back cabin of a narrow boat had to be home to the whole family but was usually kept in immaculate order; one can see that the brass of the lamp is gleaming with polish.

after the horse and that was a part of her life that she looked back on with real affection. She told a story of once, because of a hold up, having to lead a horse at night on the lonely path over a tunnel, while the boat was legged through. She was very scared, but the horse kept nuzzling up against her. 'I thought to myself, "He's telling me not to be afraid" and when I got to the end of the tunnel, I was as brave as brave.' She was kept going through the day with endless cups of very sweet tea and meals were generally plain – the three Bs – bacon, beef and beer. As she grew older, she shared the work of legging through tunnels with her brother, but while he got paid, she only got pocket money of a farthing a fortnight, an amount so small there is no modern equivalent. When she was eighteen, she got slightly less than £1 a fortnight.

Nell Cartwright had an unbelievably hard life by modern standards, yet in spite of everything, she looked back on it as an old lady with nostalgia:

I would do it all again exactly the same as I had it with the horses, the boats, the loading – I have loaded and emptied 25 tons of corned beef, I have emptied 31 tons of spelter, I have done 25 tons of timbers – to me work was nothing, I couldn't care less, I don't even today. What I would like to see now – before I leave this world – I would like to see all those horses back and the place come back as it was when I knew it.

In many ways, however, the life of the boat children was happier and healthier than that of the young children

Wash day on the canal was very basic, but the little girl in the picture looks to be enjoying her life.

Boatwomen worked every bit as hard as the men – some might say even harder. Unloading coal was tough, physical work.

working in industrial Britain. The one thing, however, that they lacked was education, being constantly on the move. One man who did try and do something about it was George Smith, a philanthropist who had himself had a hard childhood and campaigned for working children. In 1873, he started investigating the life of the boat children, and published his results in the book *Our Canal Population*. He lobbied parliament to obtain better conditions for boat children and for their education. He was successful in that two Acts were passed in 1878 and 1884. They were aimed at ensuring that the children got at least a basic education. One result was the setting up of a school in a converted boat at Brentford. It was not entirely successful; the children were always liable to be plucked out of the classroom when the family had to move on.

The lives of the boat women were as hard as those of the men, and arguably harder, as on top of the work on the boat, they were also expected to look after all the chores of cooking and cleaning. It cannot be easy trying to keep the tiny cabin immaculate, when the day has been spent unloading tons of coal. The facilities on a narrow boat were obviously limited and one item that was absent was any form of toilet. E. Temple Thurston described a trip he made with a professional boatman he referred to as Eynsham Harry, in a narrow boat in his book *The Flower of Gloster*, published in 1913. He had been worrying about how women coped without losing their modesty:

'What do the women of the barge do in such case', I asked, 'when you are miles from any cottage or place of habitation?'

The school for the children from the boats that was established in a converted barge at Brentford.

'Do?', said he, 'Why, look you, sur – that hedge which runs along every tow-path. If Nature couldn't grow enough leaves on that hedge to hid a sparrow's nest, it ain't no good to God, man, nor beast.'

I wanted no better answer than that. Where there is Nature there are no laws of decency. Not only to the physiologist, but to Nature too, all things are pure.

The horse remained the main source of power until the 1860s, when there was an attempt to develop steam powered narrow boats. They first appeared on the Grand Junction Canal, where the carrying company Fellows, Morton & Clayton ran a fleet of them. They were sophisticated, with two cylinder engines running at what was then the comparatively high pressure of 140 pounds per square inch (psi).

There were disadvantages. Valuable space was taken up by the engine, boiler and coal bunker – space that would otherwise have been available for cargo. Also, an extra man had to be employed to look after the engine. But to compensate for that, the powered boat could be used to pull an ordinary unpowered narrow boat behind it. However, the steam narrow boats were never popular. Real change only came with the next transport revolution.

One name became associated with the new means of transport, that of the Swedish engineer Erik August Bolinder. He was born in Stockholm in 1863 and as an adult joined the family firm, which he took over in 1888. In 1893, he designed a paraffin engine, but then concentrated on heavy oil engines at much the same time as Rudolf Diesel was developing the engines that still bear his name. In 1908 he produced a two-stroke engine,

The preserved steam powered narrow boat *President*. Fellows, Morton & Clayton were one of the few companies to have a fleet of these craft.

which had to be started by pre-heating in a vaporiser. This was usually done by applying a blowtorch to the vaporising bulb. Once the engine was running, the heat of combustion kept it going. But the idea of using a naked flame and an inflammable liquid in a wooden boat was alarming. The Bolinder salesmen had a novel way of reassuring the boat owners – they poured some diesel into the hold and chucked in a lighted match. Nothing happened.

The first Bolinder to reach Britain was installed in a Thames lighter, the *Travers,* in 1910, and its advantages were immediately obvious. Motorised barges and lighters soon became commonplace on London's river and before long they found their way into narrow boats as well. By 1930, 230 narrow boats had been fitted with Bolinders and their very distinctive 'pop-pop' beat

became as familiar as the clop of horses' hooves on the towpath. A rather more alarming sound was a loud backfire. By pulling a lever on the engine, the boatman could alter the firing of the fuel injector and put the engine into reverse. The great advantage of the Bolinder over the steam engine was that it did not require an extra hand to work it, everything could be controlled by the steerer. That meant that most companies had working pairs, the motor boat and the former horse boat, now known as the butty, towed behind the motor. The most obvious difference between the two boats was the tiller: where the butty retained the wooden tiller and rudder, the motor had a Z shaped metal tiller and iron rudder.

The arrival of the motor boat made a huge difference to the boating families. Now one family could work two boats instead of one – and had two cabins to live in.

BOLINDER'S OIL-ENGINES
FOR CANALS

Used by—

Fellows, Morton & Clayton, Ltd.

Grand Canal Company

Etc., Etc.

DON'T EXPERIMENT !

The **BOLINDER** has proved itself the most satisfactory unit in service on the Canals for over **TWENTY YEARS.** We have the right engine for every duty————Single Boats, Pairs of Boats, Tugs, "Wide" Barges and Craft of all Types.

BOLINDER'S COMPANY LIMITED

Coronation House,

Telephone:
Royal 3582

4, Lloyds Avenue,
London, E.C. 3.

Telegrams:
Bolinders, Fen,
London.

The Bolinder engine transformed canal traffic. These oil engines were rapidly taken up for narrow boats and barges.

Once motorboats were introduced, they could be used as part of a pair, the motor towing the unpowered boat, the butty. This pair are passing the Grand Union Canal maintenance yard at Bulborne.

One boatman recalled the days working a pair of boats. The mother generally had the motor, which was easier to steer, though she had other things to do as well. The first task was to make a mug of cocoa, which was placed on the towpath under a bridge to be picked up by the husband in the butty as he came through. That would be repeated with cups of tea throughout the day. She also had to keep an eye on the children – one boatman remembered a youngster falling off the motor and being picked up by his father on the butty by his hair and dumped on the deck.

The arrival of the butty also helped to make canal transport more economical. There had been competition from the railways throughout the second half of the nineteenth century, but that had not always been bad news for the boating companies, particularly for those working the London canals. Boats could be used to collect goods from the main line stations and move them on, often down to the dock area. A far greater threat was the arrival of motor lorries, especially immediately after the First World War, when many army surplus vehicles were being sold off cheaply. To help meet the threat, the Grand Junction bought up the Regent's Canal in 1929 to form the Grand Union – they would later add other canals. In 1934, they formed their own carrying company and they also carried out a modernisation programme to improve the various routes.

Over the years, there were accidents and dark incidents. One particularly horrifying incident involved a Pickford boat in 1839. A young woman, Christina Collins, had paid for a passage on a fly boat to go and see her husband. She was alone with the three crew and along the way she was raped, murdered and her body left in the canal. There was the inevitable public outcry that seemed to suggest that the whole boating community was full of dastardly villains. But this was very much an isolated incident. Accidents and deaths among the boating community itself seldom received any publicity of any kind. The exception was a spectacular event that happened on the Regent's Canal in 1874. One of the cargoes carried by water was gunpowder. The Royal gunpowder mill had been established at Waltham Abbey on the River Lea in the eighteenth century. The product was moved around the site in special barges, being far safer than in carts with iron-shod wheels that might create a spark with disastrous results. Shipment onwards was also made by water where possible. This was the load that was on the boat that day when, for reasons that were never discovered, it suddenly exploded when

The coming of the railways did not immediately kill off canal traffic. Here goods are being exchanged between railway and canal at King's Cross.

passing under a road bridge. The bridge was severely damaged and the crew killed. The bridge was soon repaired and presents an interesting puzzle to anyone who doesn't know the story. As generations of boats are towed down the canal, the tow ropes tend to dig grooves in the bridge abutments, which are often protected by iron plates. In this case the bridge has iron columns for support, and the grooves are there, but on the inside of the pillars, suggesting that the boats had somehow been dragged out of the water, along the towpath and dropped down the other side. The explanation is, of course, that after the accident, the pillars were reversed during the restoration. Although officially Macclesfield bridge, since that day it has generally been known as 'blow-up' bridge. Happily, such accidents were rare. But far greater damage to the canals of London were done during the Second World War.

One immediate effect of the outbreak of war was that many boatmen left for the armed forces, leaving wives and families to carry on as best they could. One partial solution was to recruit women to make up crews. Those who volunteered tended to be very middle class, most of whom had never been on a canal boat in their lives but might have mucked about in a dinghy on the Norfolk Broads. One of these was Emma Smith, who described her experiences in a book, *Maidens' Trip* (1948). She was very frank about how odd they must have seemed.

It must have been an astonishing imposition for the canal people when war brought them dainty young girls to help them mind their business, clean young eager creatures with voices so pitched as to be almost impossible to understand … For years, for generations, they had worked out their hard lives undisturbed, almost unnoticed. Then suddenly – the war; and with it descended on them these fifteen or so flighty young savages, crying out for windlasses, decked up in all manner of extraordinary clothes that were meant to indicate the marriage of hard work with romance. For the most part the boaters took it stoically.

'Blow Up' bridge on the Regent's Canal, the scene of a fatal explosion in 1874.

Women volunteers who came to work on the canals in the Second World War.

The women had badges with the initials IW that stood for Inland Waterways, but the boating community quickly decided that what they actually stood for was 'Idle Women'. But they were anything but idle and in time earned the respect of the professionals. Alan Brooks, who had been born on the boats, awarded them the ultimate tribute, when he said that by the end 'You couldn't tell them from ordinary boat people'. It was not simply that they worked as hard as the other boaters, but they faced the same dangers, especially when taking cargoes in and out of London while the city was being bombed. One crew was in City Basin on the Regent's Canal when it was hit by a rocket attack in the later years of the war, and they were fortunate to emerge alive. But they were, of course, only a small part of a much larger operation, in which canal boats and lighters were busy throughout the war years keeping essential supplies moving. Emma Smith described the scene at Limehouse, where the boats were 'packed together as close as herrings on a dish'. It was a scene of non-stop

activity, as the electric cranes moved goods from ship or lighter to the holds of the narrow boats. One lesson that was quickly learned was not to try and cook in the cabin during loading – as the load dropped, the boat tipped and so did dinner. That was only one of many lessons that had to be learned. At the end of the war, almost all the girls returned to their old lives – but one remained to become Sonia Smith, wife of a boatman.

The canals did play an important part in the war effort, in helping the movement of goods around the country and especially from the Port of London, but where 13 million tons had been moved in 1938 by 1945 that had fallen to 10 million. The end of the war also brought about a massive social change with the election of a Labour government, who began a programme of nationalisation. The majority of the canals now came under the authority of the British Transport Commission. One of the first jobs was to rationalise the system and to make out a list of priorities. Some canals had, by then, little if any commercial traffic, but others were still thought to have potential for development – among them the Grand Union from Limehouse as far as Berkhamsted. Bureaucracy likes uniformity, and it was decreed that for the narrow boats, their individual names and colourful roses and castles decoration that were a source of pride were no longer appropriate. Boats became the property of British Waterways and must be standardised. The *Daily Mirror* sent a reporter to get a boatman's opinion. 'British Waterways 279,' he snarled. 'Blue paint and yellow paint,' he growled. He spat once more and said bitterly, 'It's all a lot of bloody red tape.'

Another boatman found one of the new officials peering uninvited into his back cabin and hauled him out by the scruff of his neck. The outraged official demanded, 'Do you know who I am?' to which the boatman replied 'No and I don't … care. How would you like me to go to your house, march in the front door and start poking round your bedroom?' The boating community also had a new problem to cope with – pleasure boats, often hired by families with no experience of boating and no appreciation of the working life. Those of us who began boating in those early days were far too nervous of the long, iron working boats to attempt to get in their way. Not everyone was so accommodating. One boatman, who I'll call Fred, since what he did was strictly illegal, told the following story. He was only a teenager but was already captain of a boat. He was approaching a flight of locks on the Grand Union, when he received the good news from a boat coming down that the locks were all set with him, that is to say they were all empty so he could go straight in, but there was a pleasure boat ahead. Fred shouted to the pleasure boat to wait, but instead the lock gates were slammed shut in front of him. Fred was not about to have that; he wound up the Bolinder until flames were spouting through the chimney and rammed his way straight through the lock

When the waterways were nationalised, the narrow boats lost their traditional decoration and were given a uniform, but dull styling.

gates, terrifying the family on the pleasure boat. There was no argument about who was going first from then on. Such incidents were rare, but it was all a sign of the times, as trade steadily diminished while pleasure boating increased.

What really ended commercial trade for the narrow boats was the fierce winter of 1962-3, when the canals froze in December and boats remained locked in the ice until the spring. There was another factor at work as well. One boatman, who had regularly worked on the London runs on the Grand Union, explained how he and his wife, although they were both born to the life themselves, recognised that it would not be there for their children. If they were going to have a chance in the modern world, they would need the sort of education the boat children rarely received. They left the canals for ever. Today, only pleasure boats and trip boats are seen on these waterways. But there were two other canals constructed in the London area that are now almost forgotten.

Two Acts were passed in 1801. The first was the Grand Surrey Canal and the second the Croydon Canal. The Grand Surrey Act was for a canal that would start on the south bank of the Thames at Rotherhithe and would run as far as Mitcham, with what were very loosely described as 'divers collateral Cuts or Branches communicating from the same to certain parishes and places within the counties of Surrey and Kent'. The Croydon Canal was to join the Grand Surrey near Deptford and continue on to Croydon.

As was all too common with canal projects, the company kept having to go back to parliament either because they needed authorisation to raise more money or because the route and details kept changing. The original Act allowed for £60,000 with a further £30,000 being authorised if needed. But in 1807, they were back to parliament to get another £60,000 to complete the work. The following year, another £14,000 was agreed. The next and final Act was agreed in 1811 and came with the biggest request yet – for a massive £150,000 to complete the work. By then the company had managed to build a basin at Rotherhithe and a short stretch to the Camberwell Road. It was, however, built to generous dimensions, able to take barges up to 105ft long and 17ft 9in beam, with a draught of 4ft 9in. The investors must by now have been wondering if they'd ever see a return for their money. They were

right to be worried; they got their first dividend, a meagre 2 per cent, in 1819 which rose to 3 per cent the following year, but never got any higher.

There were suggestions for lengthening the canal, but they were never developed, largely because of the cost. The main changes occurred at the Rotherhithe end, where the dock area was increased, starting with the construction of a new lock joining the canal to the Thames to the west of the original, connecting to a new basin. Other basins were added but had to fight for trade with the nearby docks built by the Commercial Dock Company. There was, however, one regular customer. In the days before natural gas was brought to Britain, all gas was made by burning coal in retorts to produce coal gas – with coke as a side product. Gas was far more in demand then than it is now, since as well as many other uses it was the main means by which buildings and streets were lit. To meet the demand called for large quantities of coal to be delivered, and the South Metropolitan Gas Company in the Old Kent Road had its own fleet of barges with tugs to move them. Timber was also a major cargo on the canal, but the canal was never the success its promoters had hoped. The 'divers cuts and branches' were limited to a half mile long extension to Peckham and the main line never reached beyond the three and a bit miles from the Thames to Camberwell. It struggled on, but was abandoned in the 1940s when parts were filled in. The old Camberwell Basin and about a mile of canal have survived in what is now Burgess Park.

The Croydon Canal was built to a less generous scale than the Grand Surrey, with locks 60ft by 9ft. Once again, more Acts of Parliament were needed to raise money, starting with an allowance for spending £80,000, eventually another £110,000 was needed. Although the canal was only 9¼ miles long, it required a total of 28 locks. There were 26 at the start, then a long pound following the natural contours, before the final two locks lifted the canal to the basin providing a total rise of 174ft. It must have been something of a nightmare to work, but it did contain one interesting feature. Because there was no natural source of water available at the summit of the canal, water had to be pumped up to prevent the top level becoming dry – every time a lock was filled, it drained water away from the summit that had to be replaced to prevent the canal drying out. In 1830, a new pumping engine

The Surrey Canal in 1836 by G.F. Bragg. It is crossed by the newly opened London and Greenwich Railway.

was introduced. Samuel Brown was a British engineer who invented a novel kind of pumping engine, using gas. In essence, it was like the early steam engines, in which steam was condensed below a piston in a cylinder to create a vacuum at which point air pressure would push the piston down. This was connected to an overhead beam, with pump rods at the opposite end. As the piston fell, so the pump rods rose. Pressure equalised, gravity pulled the pump rods back down. In the early Smith engine, he forced air out of the cylinder by igniting gas. It is one of the earliest examples of an internal combustion engine. But Smith's gas vacuum engine was not enough to save the ailing canal. It was officially closed in 1836. A short section of the canal has survived in Betts Park in Anerley as a water feature.

It seemed that the canals and river navigations that linked into the Thames at London had seen the end of commercial trading for ever. But these days, faced with the appalling damage likely to be inflicted on the world by climate change, it remains as true today as it was when the first canal was built. It requires less effort – and therefore less fuel – to move bulk cargo by water than by land. In the context of London, water transport has an advantage, in not clogging up already overcrowded streets. So, when it came to the building of a new stadium in London to house the 2012 Olympic Games, it was decided that as far as possible, materials and people would be brought to the site by water to be unloaded directly from the Lea Navigation. Whether this trend in using water transport will continue is unlikely, and certainly the narrow canals suffer from a severe disadvantage – they are unable to take international, standard containers. But now it is time to turn the clock back again to what was an exciting new development for London: the arrival of steam powered vessels.

Barges were brought into use bringing construction material up the River Lea for the construction of the Olympic Stadium.

Photo: By permission of the Thames Ironworks
and Shipbuilding Co., Ltd.

BIRD'S-EYE VIEW OF THE THAMES
IRONWORKS SHIPBUILDING
YARD, SHOWING TWO WAR-
SHIPS UNDER CONSTRUCTION.

It is interesting to note that although steamers were being built at the yard there is still a sailing ship at the quay.

CHAPTER 5

THE STEAM AGE

There was a brief mention in the previous chapter of the earliest form of steam engine that worked by condensing steam under a piston, when air pressure forced the piston down. It was fine for pumping out coal mines where fuel was cheap, but for other users it was cripplingly expensive. The problem was that energy was being wasted by repeatedly cooling and reheating the cylinder. The solution was found by James Watt. Instead of condensing the steam in the cylinder, he used a separate condenser and could keep the cylinder permanently hot. And to preserve the heat, he closed off the top of the cylinder and, instead of air pressure, used steam pressure to move the piston. But now, he could allow steam to be introduced both above and below the cylinder, and with the piston now being moved up and down, it could be connected by a mechanism, such as a crank, to turn a wheel – and was soon finding a new use in providing power for mills and factories.

A rotary steam engine. It is not difficult to see how the flywheel could be replaced by a wheel for a paddle steamer.

For centuries, wheels had been made to turn by the force of water power – and the turning wheel could then be used through gearing to work machinery in mills. If you reversed the process and used machinery to turn a wheel with paddles and put it on a boat, then as it turned it would force the water backwards. And, according to Newton's law that every action has an equal and opposite reaction, if the water went backwards, the vessel would be forced to move forward. It would become a paddle steamer. Although steam power had been developed in Britain, the first successful paddle steamer was built in France, designed by the aristocratic Marquis Jouffroy d'Abbans. Named *Pyroscaphe* the steamer was run successfully on the River Saône in 1783. The French, however, failed to follow up the experiment, and the country was soon to be involved in a revolution that was political not industrial. The next successful attempts were made back in Britain.

William Symington built an engine that he tried out on a lake near Dumfries in 1788, and among the passengers who joined him for a jaunt on the water was Robert Burns who, alas, never wrote a verse about his experience. Symington was then commissioned to build a steam tug, the *Charlotte Dundas,* for use on the Forth and Clyde Canal. It was a very simple affair, with a single, horizontal cylinder and a connecting rod to a crank to turn the wheel, mounted in the stern. It was successful in that it hauled two 70-ton barges up the canal for twenty miles in six hours, in spite of a strong headwind. But the canal owners feared the wash would damage the canal banks and that was the end of that. The next development occurred across the Atlantic, where Robert Fulton established a regular paddle steamer service between New York and Albany. The vessel may have been American, but the engine was sent from England by Boulton and Watt.

The *Charlotte Dundas* paddle steamer was originally developed to use as a tug on the Forth & Clyde Canal, but was rejected after trials as it was feared it would damage the canal banks.

The next pioneer was to have a profound effect on the development of steam on the water. David Napier was born into the world of heavy industry. His father ran a forge and foundry, first at Dumbarton and then at Glasgow. The boy had seven years' schooling, but preferred to spend his time at the works, where there were two steam engines – one for blowing air into the furnace and the other for boring cannon. He married young and was father to fifteen children, who he usually referred to simply as 'the swarm'. He was still only twenty when he took over the business. One of the visitors to the foundry was a hotel owner from Helensburgh, Henry Bell, who had heard about the successful Fulton steamers, and had an idea that he could successfully run excursions from his hotel on the Clyde. Napier set about constructing a suitable vessel, the *Comet*, and, from his own account, struggled with some parts of the work. The boiler would have internal flues, but he had never been involved making such a thing. His first attempt was constructed from cast iron and leaked abominably, but when he turned to wrought iron, he had more success 'with the aid of a liberal supply of horse dung in getting the boiler filled'. The engine was made by John Robertson, with a vertical cylinder and side levers – the working method was not unlike that of a beam engine, except that the beams were below the cylinder head instead of above it. Originally, it had two paddle wheels at each side, but later reverted to a more conventional arrangement. It had an unusually tall, thin funnel that also acted as a mast for a sail. It was alleged to be a great success, but David Napier wryly noted that it may have been, but Bell never paid his bill. It was, however, sufficiently successful to convince Napier that there was a future in building steamers. He was to go on to make several innovations, including designing a steeple engine for use in vessels, so named because the cylinder was set at the bottom of the boat, with the working parts towering above it. In 1837, he bought a site by the Thames at Millwall to be run by his sons. A number of vessels were built by J. & F. Napier, the first of which made its way

A replica of the *Comet*, the first excursion steamer, originally sailing up the Clyde from Helensburgh.

into that very curious work, *The Ingoldsby Legends* by the Reverend Richard Barham.

> If in one of the trips of the steamboat *Eclipse*
> You should go down to Margate to look at the ships.

Napier would eventually decide that the future of shipbuilding would not be in London, but further north, where raw materials and engineering expertise were well established. The Napier family were to have a long and successful period at yards on the Clyde.

The idea of using paddle steamers for passenger excursions inspired Marc Brunel to have one built to provide excursions to Margate from London. The idea of going to the seaside for pleasure only developed in the eighteenth century, when it was thought seawater had numerous health-giving properties. So, although visitors rarely went swimming, they did bathe in tubs of seawater and even drank it. Brunel had an engine installed in a former packet boat, the *Regent*, and it made its first voyage from London Bridge in 1813 with Brunel himself on board. When he arrived in Margate, the owner of the York Hotel refused to let him have a room as he strongly disapproved of the new type of vessel. Passengers, fortunately, did not share his disapproval. Encouraged by this success, Brunel considered other uses for paddle steamers. He suggested to the Admiralty that steam tugs would be a valuable addition to the fleet in bringing sailing vessels into and out of ports. The Admiralty were not impressed:

> Their Lordships feel it their bounden duty to discourage the employment of steam vessels as they consider the introduction of steam is calculated to strike a fatal blow at the naval superiority of the Empire.

Ship building did, however, develop very rapidly right down the Thames from Limehouse, all round the Isle of Dogs to the mouth of the River Lea. One company, specialising in constructing engines, deserves a special mention, because of its connections right back to the early years of steam power. Joseph Miller was born in 1797 and the godfather at his christening was none

The man-of-war *Dreadnought* being towed up the Thames by a steam paddle tug.

other than James Watt. The boy later trained at the Soho works of Boulton & Watt and he was to go into partnership with another Soho trainee, John Barnes. In 1822 these two young men set up in business for themselves at Glasshouse Fields, just to the west of the mouth of the River Lea. In 1826, they built the engine for a 256-ton paddle steamer, *Sophia Jane*. That in itself was not remarkable, but what is surprising is to find this comparatively small craft setting out slowly chugging its way round the world, with many stops en route, to eventually arrive in Australia. Up to then, most steamers had been designed for comparatively short trips. But engineers were dreaming of greater things. One of the best-known stories of these early days is that

when Isambard Kingdom Brunel was questioned about whether it was really possible to build a railway line all the way from London to Bristol, he simply answered – why stop there, why not go on to New York. We will never know whether he meant to be taken seriously or not, but he was by a member of the Great Western Railway board, Thomas Guppy. The result was the formation of the Great Western Steamship Company, with the object of making a crossing of the Atlantic using only steam power. The work was to be controlled by a committee consisting of Brunel, Guppy, a former naval Captain 'Christopher Claxton' and another GWR stalwart, Peter Maze. The ship was to be built in Bristol by William Patterson.

Isambard Kingdom Brunel's ship the SS *Great Western*: she was fitted out with engines built in London.

One paddle steamer, the American *Savannah*, had made an Atlantic crossing, but she was fitted with specially designed retractable paddle wheels and spent most of the voyage under sail. It was such a new event that, in the course of the voyage, the captain of a sailing ship spotted what he thought was a ship on fire, and set sail to the rescue, only to discover it was smoke from the funnel of the gently chugging steamer. The general opinion was that an Atlantic crossing using only steam power was impossible. Dr Dionysus Lardner, an eminent scientist notable for having his predictions proved wrong, argued that no vessel could carry enough fuel to make the journey practical. Increasing the size would make no difference, because a ship twice as big would need twice as much fuel. There was a fundamental flaw in his argument. The amount of fuel needed depends on overcoming the resistance of the water and is proportional to the area of the hull – not the volume. To put it in simplest terms one measurement depends on the square of the dimensions, the volume is a cubic measure. This was obvious to Brunel, but he was not alone in planning a steam powered crossing. There was another new company – the British-American Steam Navigation Company – which also had their eye on being the first to win the honour of steaming the Atlantic. They had placed an order for a vessel, initially known as the *Victoria*, with the London ship builders, Cox and Curling at Limehouse.

There was a problem that faced all shipbuilders at the start of the steam age. While they were expert in providing the wooden ships, they had neither the expertise nor the machinery to construct the engines. This was true of both Cox and Curling and Patterson in Bristol. The London company had ordered the engines from Girdwood and Sons of Glasgow, but the company went bankrupt, which meant that they had to start again with a new firm. This time they turned to the reliable Napier company to do the job. But the inevitable delays meant that there was no chance of the ship being ready in time to beat the Brunel ship now under construction in Bristol, the *Great Western*. Brunel also had to have the engines made separately and he turned to the ever-reliable company of Maudsley Field and Son. That meant the vessel had to be towed down to London for fitting out and having her engines installed.

The British-American company were still keen to be the first to make the Atlantic crossing. There was no chance that the *Victoria* would be ready on time, so they acquired a two-masted paddle steamer *Sirius* normally employed on runs between London, Plymouth and Cork. She was brought down to London as well to be prepared for the long voyage. Now there were two vessels on the Thames getting ready for the contest. On 28 March 1838, as the *Great Western* was getting ready for her sea trials, Brunel was surprised to find *Sirius* on her way down river, not for a trial but heading for Cork, where she was to take on fuel before setting off for New York. The Bristol party were not too alarmed as they knew their ship was considerably faster than their smaller rival. They set off for Bristol on 31 March, but they had scarcely got under way when fire broke out in the forward boiler room. It did not cause any serious structural damage, but in his eagerness to see for himself what was happening, Brunel started down the ladder to go below where the fire was burning. But a rung had collapsed in the heat and the engineer fell. Had he landed on the deck below he would have been unlikely to have survived, but instead he fell on top of Captain Claxton. Brunel was taken off, injured but lucky to be alive.

The *Great Western* was ready to leave Bristol on 7 April, but was held in harbour by bad weather for an extra day. Then came the disheartening news; *Sirius* had left Cork four days earlier and theirs was a shorter crossing. So inevitably, the honour of being the first ship to cross the Atlantic using steam power for the entire voyage, went to the little *Sirius*. The *Great Western* was not far behind, having been gaining on her rival by averaging two knots a day faster speed. But that was not what made this race for prestige important. When *Sirius* arrived, her coal bunkers were almost empty – there were even rumours that the crew had been taking off cabin doors to feed the furnaces. The *Great Western* however had 200 tons of coal left. The point had been resoundingly made; when it came to long voyages by steamers, bigger really was best. This was a fact that was about to lead to a revolution in ship building. It led to a greater demand for special marine steam engines, and the largest iron works in London – the Canal Iron Works in Millwall – specialised in this work and continued manufacturing them up to 1882.

It was all very well realising that the answer to the Atlantic trade was to build ever bigger ships, but there are limits to the size of a wooden hull. Brunel

The SS *Sirius* was the first ship to cross the Atlantic using steam power all the way, arriving just before the *Great Britain.*

Casting the cylinder for a marine steam engine at The Canal Iron Works in Milwall.

had the answer; his next ship would be built with an iron hull. It was not a new idea. The first iron-hulled vessel to arrive in London was the *Aaron Manby* built in Tipton on the Birmingham Canal system. The yard was owned by Charles Manby, who had taken out a patent for iron steamships. She was not a huge vessel – 180ft long by 17ft wide – but too large to fit into the British canal system. So the vessel had to be sent to London in sections for assembly and in 1822, work completed, she set off down the Thames for Le Havre, then on again to Paris. Others soon followed. William Fairbairn had originally trained as a millwright but became interested in the structural use of iron. He began building small iron ships in sections at Manchester, but in 1835 he moved to London and established a works at Millwall. His first vessel – another *Sirius* – was a modest 180 tons but was the first iron steamer to be built on the Thames. Fairbairn also had a part to play in another engineering first. Robert Stephenson was the engineer in charge of constructing a railway to Holyhead, that would involve a crossing of the Menai Straits. Thomas Telford had crossed the Straits with a suspension bridge, but that was not considered either appropriate or safe for a bridge carrying heavy locomotives and rolling stock. He went to see Fairbairn and together they carried out a series of tests, eventually coming up with a novel solution. The bridge would be like a box girder, made up of riveted wrought iron plates. But where girders are simply supports, the iron tubes would be big enough for the trains to run on rails inside them. The whole construction process used the technology that Fairbairn was using at Millwall, and a 75ft scale model was built at the yard and tested there. The actual components of the bridge, that were assembled on site in Wales, were made at another Thames shipyard, C.J. Mare at Blackwall. It is fair to say that the successful construction of what became known as the Britannia Bridge was very much the product of the shipyards of London.

Brunel's second ship is not really part of the London story, but it had such a profound effect on the future of shipbuilding that it has to be looked at. As originally planned, it was to be a paddle steamer with engines designed by F. Humphreys. A problem at once appeared; no forge in the country could deal with producing the great crankshaft. The difficulty was overcome by James Nasmyth, who promptly designed a steam hammer – he sketched it out the day he was first consulted. In this case, the hammer head was raised in a vertical frame using steam power and then allowed to fall back under gravity – in later models, steam was also used to give extra impetus to the hammer. It was to become an essential piece of equipment for shipyards throughout Britain. Scarcely had the crankshaft problem been solved than it became redundant. Brunel had heard about experiments made by Francis Pettit Smith in using a screw propeller and had installed one on an experimental craft, *Archimedes*. Having studied the working of the new machinery, Brunel decided to scrap his paddle wheels and use the new propeller. It was a bitter blow for the young designer Humphreys, whose engine design was now thrown out. He died shortly afterwards. The SS *Great Britain* was to set a new standard for shipbuilding. Paddle steamers would continue to be built right up to the middle of the twentieth century, but mostly for use in coastal waters. For world shipping, the industry would increasingly become dominated by iron-hulled ships, driven by screw propellers.

In 1856, C.J. Mare, who had provided the ironwork for the Britannia Bridge, were struggling and the company was taken over by Mare's father-in-law Peter Rolt and renamed the Thames Ironworks & Shipbuilding Company. The company was to have a long and generally successful history. As the name suggests, they made their own iron plates and angle irons from melted down scrap metal. The site would have had a cacophony of sounds, much of it coming from the riveters. In the process, the rivets, which were basically like round-headed bolts, were heated in a brazier to almost white heat. The iron plates to be fastened together would have been previously drilled, so that holes aligned. The rivet was pushed through the two sheets. One man, on the outside of the hull, held the rivet firmly in place, while on the other side of the plates it was hammered until the protruding end of the rivet was flattened out to hold them firmly together. In a busy yard, there would be riveters at work all over the hull, banging metal on metal. Readers will not be surprised to learn that many riveters suffered from deafness in later life.

The company built both passenger steamers and warships. The best-known example of their work was Britain's first ever ironclad battleship HMS *Warrior*. The need for such a ship only really developed with the introduction of rifled guns firing shells to replace the old cannon and cannon balls. It was obvious that shells

The author standing beside the propeller of the SS *Great Britain*: the first transatlantic vessel to use a propeller instead of paddle wheels.

could do immense damage to a wooden hull, but the Admiralty showed no sense of urgency in developing any form of protection against the new weapons. It was only when the French started building up their own formidable fleet that they sat up and took notice. Dupuy de Lôme had a position in the French Navy equivalent to the British Surveyor of the Navy. In 1859, he designed a battleship, the *Gloire,* that had iron sheets attached to the outside of the hull. He declared that the appearance of his ship in amongst a fleet of wooden walls would be like having a lion in a flock of sheep. The Admiralty tended to agree with him and at once put the design of an ironclad battleship at the top of their list of priorities.

An ordinary iron hull offered little protection: indeed, a shell passing through could cause huge devastation, sending metal splinters flying in every direction. The solution was to build the ship with a conventional iron hull. Attached to the outside of that was a layer of

teak, 18 inches thick, and beyond that was a 4½-inch thick layer of wrought iron plates. That was not the only innovative feature of the ship. Her engines were designed and built by another London engineer and shipbuilder, John Penn & Sons of Greenwich.

John Penn the elder was a millwright, who set up in business for himself at Greenwich in 1800. His first connection with marine affairs came when he was asked to provide the machinery for the bakery at the Deptford Victualling Yard. Then in 1822, he and his teenage son, also called John, went to see the *Aaron Manby*. It was not so much the iron hull that impressed them as the oscillating steam engine, and they set up in business making marine engines. The elder Penn died in 1843 and his son took over. The engine he designed for *Warrior* was a trunk engine. The 'trunk' is a hollow piston rod, and unlike the usual engines where the connecting rod is fastened to the end of the piston rod, in this case the

A bulkhead on the armour-plated HMS *Warrior* showing how protection was provided against shells by sandwiching timber between iron plates.

connecting rod is inside the trunk. The piston rod itself is either cast with the piston or bolted to it. It was very compact, and the whole engine could be placed low down in the ship, below the water line. This made it ideal for a warship, where it would be protected from direct hits by shell fire, hence the choice of the Penn engine for *Warrior*.

Although modern in many ways, in other ways she was still looking back to an earlier tradition. She carried a full set of sails, which did at least have the advantage that if speed was essential, they could be used together with the engine. Under steam alone she had a speed of around 14 knots, but on a run from Portsmouth to Plymouth under sail and steam she reached 17.5 knots.

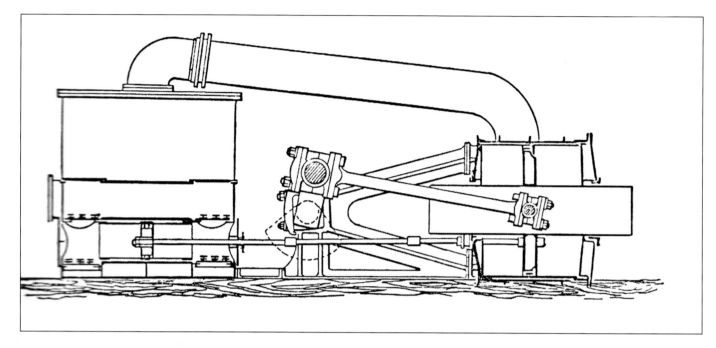

The Penn trunk engine designed for HMS *Warrior*.

Her armaments were all arranged down the sides, only able to deliver broadsides just as in the days of Nelson's navy. It seemed for a time that the pioneering ironclad would have an ignominious end as a hulk, but she was rescued and restored to look as she would have been after her launch in 1861. She is now on display with two other iconic vessels, *Victory* and *Mary Rose*, at Portsmouth.

Both Penn and the Thames Company went on to further successes. John Penn worked with Francis Pettit Smith on improving the bearings of propeller shafts, which may sound of minor importance, but the old-style bearings wore out quickly and there was always the risk of them giving out before a voyage was complete. The Penn works were impressive. The main engine works were at Blackheath Hill and the boiler works at Deptford and a shuttle service between the two was run by traction engines. There was a huge engine assembly shop, five steam hammers and machines for casting, boring and planning. One job that came their way must have seemed of minor importance to a ship builder in the 1870s. The Aeronautical Society was trying to experiment with the idea of developing heavier than air flying machines. They reasoned that the effect created by an aeroplane travelling at speed through still air could be replicated by having a model aeroplane motionless and thrusting air past it at high speed. They developed

the wind tunnel, and the very first was built by Penn's. In 1899, the company amalgamated with the Thames Company. In its latter years, the Thames company was under the management of Arnold Hills, who joined the Board in 1880. His most notable achievement was to restore sound industrial relations to the company. There had been a strike in July 1897 that lasted right through to the following February, during which the yard was kept going by employing blackleg labour. It had involved the employers' organisation as a whole – the Federation of British Shipbuilders – but at the end of it, Hills was disillusioned with the arrangements. He withdrew from the Federation and negotiated directly with his own workforce. He was able to win their support through a profit-sharing scheme, and for an industry that had become notorious for strikes, his yard remained untroubled. There was, however, a far greater threat to the yard: competition from the yards of Northern England and Scotland. Hills complained that his competitors were putting in lower bids to try and maintain a monopoly, but to no avail: the yard closed in 1912. The Company did have a subsidiary – the Boatbuilding Section. As the name suggests, they began by building boats, such as pinnaces and cutters. But in 1896 they reached an agreement with the Royal National Lifeboat Institution to build all their boats, and between then and the closure they produced 206 lifeboats and

HMS *Warrior* has been restored and is now open to the public in Portsmouth.

must certainly have helped to save many, many lives at sea. The lifeboat story will be told in more detail later.

Part of the design of *Warrior* was the work of John Scott Russell. He was one of the great innovators in nineteenth-century shipbuilding. Early in his career, he worked for a company making vessels that took passengers along the two canals linking Glasgow and Edinburgh. He studied how to overcome the resistance that barges faced by building up waves in comparatively narrow waterways – these were the waterways on which the *Charlotte Dundas* had been tried out. He also developed a new method of strengthening hulls, by means of longitudinal stiffeners combined with regularly spaced bulkheads. The former experiments led to his 'wave theory' of ship design, which, though flawed, did lead to some elegant vessels being constructed.

The longitudinal strengthening was to prove crucial for large ships.

In 1847, he and partners took over the former Fairbairn yard on the Thames. One of his first commissions was for a yacht, *Titania*, for Robert Stephenson. For the railway engineer it was somewhere where he could get away from the incessant calls on his time – he referred to it as the home that had a door with no knocker. She was raced against the yacht *America* – a race that inaugurated the America's Cup. It may have been Stephenson's enthusiasm for his yacht that impressed his friend and fellow engineer, Isambard Brunel. The engineer was now planning a third ship that would be far larger than his previous two vessels – too big to be built in Bristol. She was in fact far bigger than any vessel ever built at that time at 692ft long with an 82ft beam and four decks.

She was so large that she was equipped with both paddle wheels and a propeller, with four steam engines for the paddles and one for the propeller. She was designed for the long sea voyage to Australia via India.

The seeds of discontent were sown at the very start of the project. Brunel had made his own cost estimates of a total of £275,200 for the hull, which did not include the cost of engines and boilers, which would be a separate contract. Scott Russell offered to take on the building contract for £258,000 on condition that he was also given the option of building a planned sister ship. If there is one thing that engineering history shows time and time again it is the fallibility of estimates; there were cases where projects came in under cost, but they were rare compared to the vast number that finished up far more expensive. This was particularly true when the project involved totally new ideas, as was the case here. Brunel, however, must have been delighted to find such a respected ship builder confident enough to make

the offer, which he was happy to accept. The contract was drawn up specifying exactly what was needed and including a clause that probably seemed unimportant at the time, but which was to have an effect on the whole project – the contractor was also responsible for bearing the costs of the launch.

Scott Russell would have been used to the client asking him to build the ship and then after his designs had been approved, he would have expected to be left alone to get on with it. But now he had Brunel to contend with and the contract was quite clear:

> All calculations, drawings, models and templates which the contractor may prepare shall from time to time be submitted to the Engineer for his revision and alteration or approval. The Engineer to have entire control over the proceedings and the workmanship.

It was never going to be an easy relationship.

Brunel's last ship, the *Great Eastern*, under construction on the Thames: unlike most vessels, she is being constructed parallel to the river, instead of at right angles to it.

Quite early on, word started to be put around that Scott Russell was the real designer, and that Brunel had done little more than come to him and say – 'please build me a big ship. I leave the details to you.' When news of this came to Brunel, he was livid and made it quite clear that the whole project 'originated with me, and has been worked out by me at a great cost of labour and thought devoted to it now for not less than three years'. The actual work occupied two yards, the Russell yard and the adjoining yard, recently vacated by David Napier. At first, things went well with the construction, but costs kept mounting. Russell ran out of funds, and it was agreed to advance him ten instalments of £8,000 each, provided an agreed schedule of work was carried out. Then a major row erupted between the two men regarding how the great vessel was to be launched. Scott Russell wanted it launched bow first into the river, but Brunel vetoed the idea, demanding it was launched

sideways. For the cash-strapped ship builder this was more than a disagreement about method. He had signed a contract that stated he had to pay for the launch – and that Brunel had the ultimate decision on how it was to be done. The result was inevitable; Scott Russell went bankrupt. It then emerged that he had mortgaged his own yard and that it now belonged to his creditors. The Steamship Company now had to begin negotiations to get access to the half of the ship that now lay on someone else's property. Prices were agreed, but the rents were immense.

The vessel was finally ready, and the launch began on 3 November 1857. Brunel had requested that there should be no spectators and that everything should be done quietly and in an orderly fashion to his direction. But the Company, anxious to recoup some of the rising costs, sold tickets for the event. The result was more chaotic than orderly and as a result, there was a fatal

Preparing for the launch of the *Great Eastern* with men standing by the restraining drums that were to control the descent of the vessel down the slipway.

accident when one of the workmen was hit by a winch handle on the mechanism that controlled the restraining chains. There had to be more than one attempt to get the vast ship into the water, which could only be done at the high Spring tide period. Eventually the task was completed on 31 January the following year. The ship was never the successful passenger vessel that had been hoped, but she did go on to prove invaluable in laying telegraph cables around the world. But controversy has never left the ship; how much of the design really was down to Scott Russell and was the bankruptcy brought about by Brunel's constantly making changes or had the shipbuilder got his estimates wildly wrong? Whatever the truth of the matter, it did nothing to dent Scott Russell's reputation, who went on to build more ships. For Brunel, it was his last project. His health deteriorated and he died in 1859.

It is not possible to give details of every single yard that worked along the Thames, but two deserve special mention. Alfred Yarrow was, it seems, an inventor from the start. As a young boy, he got bored holding skeins of wool for an enthusiastically knitting aunt, so devised a machine for the job. He was expected to go upstairs to the top of the house every night to make sure his grandmother had put her candle out. He rigged up a device where the candle snuffer was held by a thread attached to her pillow, so when her head went down the candle went out. While still at school he rigged up a private electric telegraph to a friend's house. It was no surprise that as an adult his inventions continued – starting with a steam carriage that bowled along at a respectable 25mph. Then, in 1863, he raised £1,000 to set up in business with a boat repair yard on the Isle of Dogs. His partner Hedley was said to have good

The grandiose main saloon of the *Great Eastern*. Although she was never a success as a passenger liner, she had an extremely useful working life laying undersea telegraphy cables.

connections, but the first year they lost £100 and the following year £1,000. Yarrow had once worked on a steam launch, so he decided to forget repair work and concentrate on building launches. He put out an advert and got an order for a launch that cost £200 to build but sold for just £145. But the following year he brought it back for £100 and sold it on again for £200. He took a photo of the launch, had copies made, and took them to pubs up and down the Thames. Between 1868 and 1875, they built 150 launches, after which he split with Hedley. All this would have been of minor importance in the world at large, but everything changed thanks to developments in America.

During the American Civil War, a Confederate officer, Captain Hunter Davidson, invented the spar torpedo. It was an explosive charge at the end of a long pole – intrepid sailors used it attached to a rowing boat that charged at the target – and then the crew rowed back as fast as they could and with luck didn't get blown up as well. Yarrow argued that a steam launch would get away far faster than a rowing boat and started experimenting with torpedo boats. But then, in 1877, Robert Whitworth developed the self-propelling torpedo – and that Yarrow decided was the perfect weapon to use with his steam launches. He was soon building torpedo boats for countries from Argentina to Japan, but not yet for the Royal Navy. The Admiralty was, as usual, slow to adapt to the new technology. Yarrow had received orders for boats from Russia, but these were cancelled when war broke out with Turkey, so he offered them to the Admiralty. They baulked at the price at first, but eventually agreed provided they could insert a clause stipulating that the price would drop for every knot the vessels dropped below a speed of 18 knots. Yarrow agreed on condition that the price should also increase for every knot above the figure. He had, in fact, been experimenting with improving the propeller and as a result in trials the craft reached

Yarrow's yard on the Isle of Dogs, where they began building steam launches in 1865.

21.9 knots. It was the start of a lucrative business. At the same time, he recognised that his vessels were a new threat to naval vessels, and that could only be countered by having equally fast warships to engage them. In 1892, he designed two vessels, *Havock* and *Hornet,* each 180ft long and 18ft beam that reached speeds of over 27 knots, thanks in large measure to a new boiler design. They were the first of a new class of warship – the destroyer.

A similar path was followed by John Isaac Thorneycroft, whose parents were both sculptors: Thomas Thorneycroft was responsible for one of London's best-known works, the statue of Boadicea on the Thames embankment. Fortunately, Thomas also had an interest in engineering and taught his son metal working. John was just nineteen when he built his first steam launch in 1862 – the first on the river that was able to keep up with the crews in the Oxford-Cambridge boat race. He trained in naval architecture, and with his father's financial help set up a launch building business at Chiswick. Like Yarrow, he became interested in developing vessels to use the spar torpedo. He gave a dramatic demonstration of his new torpedo boat for the French navy, using an old warship 'the *Bayonnaise*' as the

target. The vessel struck the ship at full force, creating a hole described as being 'as big as a house'. The torpedo boat rebounded fifteen metres, then steamed away unharmed. Thorneycroft realised that if he was going to move on from simply building small vessels, he would have to leave Chiswick where he was separated from the sea by a succession of low bridges and he moved to Southampton to build larger vessels with great success. They continued building launches on the Thames right up to 1909.

The Chiswick yard was among the last builders on the Thames. By the start of the First World War, ship building had come to an end, but during a long history the yards along the river had produced a vast number of vessels and pioneered many new developments. The arrival of steam also produced dramatic changes to the working life of the Thames. Steam tugs were introduced that could take over the task of hauling heavy lighters and barges. They were also to prove valuable in towing large sailing vessels as they made their way between the open sea and the port of London. Earlier in the chapter we mentioned Marc Brunel's steamer offering excursions from London. When he returned to Margate a few years

A Thorneycroft steam torpedo boat built for the Spanish Navy in the 1890s.

The steam paddle tug *Ben More* on the Thames. The lack of any sort of wheelhouse must have made for many chilly winter passages for the steerer.

One of the important jobs carried out by steam tugs was towing sailing ships down the Thames estuary. This illustration from William Armstrong's book *The Thames* shows a busy scene at Fiddlers' Reach.

An excursion steamer by the Thames Embankment from an old postcard.

later, he found that his modest steamer was now just one of a large fleet offering excursions to the seaside resorts of the south east. The piers that have now become such iconic features of many resorts were originally built to allow passengers to get straight off the pleasure boats, without having to be rowed ashore. Steamers not only took visitors round the coast, they also took them for excursions up and down the river. Today, visitors rarely have a chance actually to travel by steam power on the Thames, but the world's last sea-going paddle steamer *Waverley* does still make an annual visit to the city as a reminder of the great days of steam.

CHAPTER 6

LONDON DOCKS

Traffic on the river increased throughout the eighteenth century to the extent that overcrowding of the Pool became a major problem. Theoretically, the maximum number of vessels that could be moored was around 550, but when a count was taken in 1794, 800 vessels were moored, sometimes as many as 16 abreast. The situation was intolerable, and it was clear that something needed to be done, and a whole series of different proposals were put forward. The merchants who had a vested interest in improving the facilities were the first to come out with some new ideas. William Vaughan, a director of the Royal Exchange Assurance Corporation, wrote a thesis on docks, quays and warehouses in 1793, in which he favoured the construction of docks, possibly at Rotherhithe or the Isle of Dogs, but his first choice was Wapping, being closer to the city centre. The idea was taken up by a committee set up to look at the whole problem and a feasibility study was made, followed by a full survey. The surveyor, Daniel Alexander, produced his report by the end of 1794, which called for two docks – to be known as 'London Docks' – at Wapping, together with a 2¾ mile long ship canal to the river at Blackwall.

They were not the only ones making plans. The Corporation of London set up its own committee in 1794, but their first suggestions were for modest changes, involving no more than improving existing quays. This was never going to be sufficient, and two years later a triumvirate of George Dance, the City Surveyor, with his engineering assistant John Foulds and the eminent canal engineer, William Jessop, was appointed to develop ideas for improving the facilities. Dance was an unusual man in that, apart from his professional life, he was also a gifted artist and a Royal Academician. In fact, he found time, during the long discussions on docks and quays, to do a portrait of Jessop. By May 1796, they had come up with four proposals that included improving the Legal Quays and wharfs and building docks at Rotherhithe and on the Isle of Dogs. They made no specific recommendations as to which was the best option, since these were only sketched out ideas that would require far more detailed examination before any sensible decision could be made.

The least ambitious plan simply called for jetties to be extended from the river wall, with new warehousing and quays to be added on the south bank. Jessop proposed a 100 acre dock at Rotherhithe, specifically for colliers and one of similar size on the Isle of Dogs for timber. As coal and timber don't need to be stored in warehouses, these would be comparatively cheap to construct. But others were already coming up with bolder plans. Ralph Walker had been a ship captain and later plantation owner in Jamaica, who had then settled in London. He put forward plans for a dock at Wapping and a proposal for a ship canal across the Isle of Dogs. Samuel Wyatt, who is best known as an architect and whose works included the Albion Mill, London's first steam-powered mill, came forward with the idea of large docks on the Isle of Dogs. Next, the engineer Joseph Hodgkinson proposed dredging the river to create a wider channel from Deptford up to London Bridge, with improved wharfs. The City eventually put forward a petition to parliament, combining various elements – extending the Legal Quays, constructing the canal across and building new docks on the Isle of Dogs.

To add to the complications, a number of West India merchants, who had previously favoured Wapping, now recognised that Blackwall offered a better prospect. It was further from the city centre, but it had deep water access, land was cheaper, and it provided an opportunity to build really extensive docks with ample warehousing. It appealed to the City, since it would mean that the biggest ships would no longer be cluttering up the Pool. This seemed a sensible plan, and once again Dance and Jessop were called in by the City to work with Ralph Walker to do a thorough investigation, that would include surveying the proposed site, taking soundings and making test borings of the ground. The result was a specific proposal for two linked docks of 21 and 10 acres, with an entrance basin at Limehouse and a lock at Blackwall. The larger of the two docks was for imported goods and was to have extensive warehousing all down one side, while the smaller was for export. The canal across the Isle of Dogs was also included in the plan and was to have a depth of 23ft and a width at water level of

176ft, more than enough for the vessels of the day. This seemed to be far and away the best scheme available and just when everything seemed settled, yet another plan was put forward, this time for replacing London Bridge by a new one that would allow large ships to travel much further upriver. Inevitably, this meant a new committee and new enquiries, but it was roundly condemned.

Eventually, when all the various schemes had been considered, a whole set of new schemes were approved by Act of Parliament in 1799. Starting upstream at Wapping, were the London Docks, 20 acres in all with an entrance lock of 150ft by 40ft and a total area of 20 acres, then came the much bigger West India Docks, with the lock 193ft by 45ft and 54 acres and at Blackwall, the East India docks, with 210ft by 47ft lock and 26 acres. The City Canal across the Isle of Dogs was also approved, with the same lock size as the West India Dock.

William Jessop was appointed engineer in charge of the canal construction. It was a major undertaking. The land of the Isle of Dogs lies 6ft below the highest water on the spring tide and was protected by sea walls. But to avoid flooding, the canal had to be constructed on an embankment – which was to be 12ft above the highwater mark to ensure safety. The bank was made up of gravel from the excavation with a core of puddled clay – that is clay mixed with water and then stamped firmly down to form a waterproof barrier. The works were kept drained during construction by means of a 15 horsepower Boulton & Watt steam engine. The canal was opened in December 1805 and was able to take ships of up to 500 tons, and would save them the long, looping trip round the Isle. Jessop was also the engineer for the West India Dock, when work started on the Import Dock in 1800. This was another immense undertaking. The dock itself was to be 23ft deep, with the quay walls rising 6ft above that. The brick walls were 6ft thick at the top, above which were massive coping stones. Strengthening buttresses were bound to the walls by iron. The walls were backed by puddled clay to reduce seepage and a one foot thick layer of clay covered the bottom of the dock. Two steam

Ships in the City Canal that cut across the Isle of Dogs in 1824.

engines were ordered from Boulton & Watt, a large 28 horsepower engine with a 36-inch diameter cylinder to keep the works drained and a 20 horsepower engine for grinding mortar.

There were many design decisions to be taken as the work went on. Jessop was always a very modest man, and always willing to give up his own idea if someone came up with a better one. He had planned conventional lifting bridges across the locks, but when he saw an alternative in October 1801, he wrote to the Chairman:

I should have before you tomorrow a specification and advertisement for the Drawbridges but I beg leave to postpone it as Mr. Walker showed me last Evening a Sketch for a design which he is preparing for a turning Bridge which I like much better than my own if, consistent with facility of opening and shutting, it is capable of having a firm abutment.

There was one tragedy. The workings were protected by coffer dams, and about thirty men were at work, digging away the earth behind one of them on the evening of 22 July 1802 when at high water the dam suddenly burst. Warning was given and most scrambled clear, but Richard Bough, the superintendent of the work, and five others died. There was no great damage done to the workings as a whole, but the reason for the collapse was never really established. In spite of the tragedy, the Import Dock was officially opened with great ceremony on 23 August. Estimates of the numbers who came to watch varied wildly from 10,000 to 30,000 and they were able to watch the first West Indiaman enter the dock to the accompaniment of a 21-gun salute. The *European Magazine* account was fulsome in its praise:

Whoever has enjoyed the satisfaction of visiting and viewing the work in its present state, must be astonished at the stupendousness of its scale, and

The opening of the West India Dock in 1802. While the highly decorated warship fires a salute, a team of men haul another vessel out of the dock.

the extent of human, skill, and industry, which has begun, carried on and so far completed in the course of five and twenty months, an 'imperial work', the proof of past and pledge of future prosperity … The warehouses are the grandest, the most commodious, and spacious, that we have seen.

The work could now be started on the smaller Export Dock and by 1806 the whole of the docks area was open for business. The total cost, including land purchase and construction of the docks and all the warehouses, came to £1,227,000. It was a great deal of money but with the income staying steady at around £200,000 year after year and with dividends regularly reaching 10 per cent, it had proved a highly profitable venture. Most of the warehouse space was devoted to the main products of the West Indies, sugar and rum, and a smaller area for cotton.

There was a perennial problem along the river of pilfering from the open wharfs, which could be reduced by building a totally enclosed dock area. There was a further incentive to build in this style when the Warehouse Act of 1823 allowed goods to be stored duty free in secure bonded warehouses. A proposal was put forward for creating a new dock close to the Tower of London. There was a certain amount of opposition to having commercial docks so close to the city, but the plan was approved by parliament, and the task of designing and overseeing construction went to two very able men. The engineer was to be Thomas Telford, who had begun his engineering career under the guidance of William Jessop some thirty years earlier. He was responsible for the actual dock. The job of designing the surrounding warehouses went to Philip Hardwick. He is best known for his later work, particularly at Euston station, where he designed the splendid neoclassical arch at the entrance, destroyed in the twentieth century by official vandals, who considered it too old fashioned for a modern station. The dock took its name from the St. Katharine's

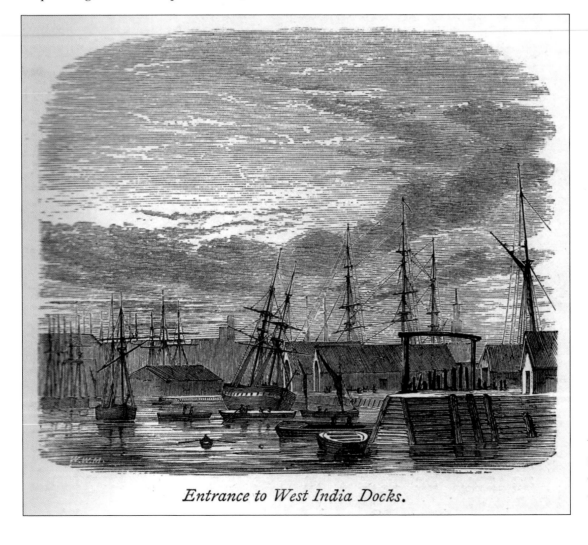

Entrance to West India Docks.

The West India Dock in the mid-nineteenth century, with ships, a Thames barge and lighters.

Hospital that had originally occupied part of the site. The site also contained around 1,000 homes, which were bought by compulsory purchase and demolished. Telford had estimated construction costs at £242,000 but purchasing the land cost a staggering £1,353,000.

In spite of the sums spent on land, there was not all that much of it and the site itself was awkward. Hardwick did his part, by designing warehouses that maximised the space. The ground floors were set back from the edge of the quays, but the upper stories overhung the quay, supported on iron pillars. That left Telford to worry about the rest of the scheme, a problem he described in his autobiography:

> When the space necessary for warehouses and entrances was subtracted 10 acres only remained for the actual docks – It being obvious that the accommodation required could not be obtained by the simple forms of squares and parallelograms. I was from necessity, led to adapt the shape of the docks to that of the ground: and this was so managed, after attentive consideration, as to become really advantageous, as affording an increased extent of wharfage and two docks instead of one.

Once work began, a coffer dam was built to allow work to continue below river level, and piling engines were brought in. It took a whole day to drive just one of the massive timbers, each 1ft square, down to a depth of 44ft through solid clay. The first stone was laid on 3 May 1827. A Swedish visitor, Captain Carlsund, described the scene. He saw 1,000 men at work, railways laid for horse-drawn waggons to move the spoil, a steam engine to keep the area clear of water and a temporary jetty to allow spoil to be removed by barge. As the excavation got deeper, barrow runs were used. These were devices Telford knew well from his canal work in deep cuttings. Basically, they consisted of planks set at an angle from the workings to the top of the excavation. Horses at the top of the runs, were attached to the full barrows, which they drew to the surface, while the navvy balanced the barrow in front of him. Once emptied, he ran back down the greasy run. It was never a job for the faint-hearted.

One problem for Telford was finding a means of keeping the basin full and supplying the entrance lock with water at a good rate. He installed an 80 horsepower Boulton & Watt steam pumping engine, which together with the conventional sluice, filled the lock in just five minutes. A second engine was used to refill the basin

St. Katharine's Dock under construction. The sketch shows a steam engine house and the barrow runs used to take spoil to the surface.

every time a ship left. Everything went ahead at great speed – rather too quickly for Telford's liking and he complained about 'such haste, pregnant as it was, and ever will be, with risks'. In fact, there was only one serious incident when, at a particularly high tide, the site was flooded, but fortunately with no loss of life. Telford need not have worried; all went well and on 25 October 1828, the first ship entered the basin, just three years after the Act was passed. It is one of the few docks in Britain that retain much of their original character.

The emphasis so far has been on activity on the north bank of the river, but the south bank has always had its share of trade and was home to the naval base at Deptford. The Rotherhithe area was largely marshy wasteland and though not much use for anything else, was ideal for creating docks. The first commercial dock was the Howland Great Dock, completed in 1699 and named after the landowner John Howland who had given the land to Wriothesley Russell, the Marquis of Tavistock as a wedding present when he married Howland's daughter. The dock was roughly 1,000ft long, 500ft wide and 17ft deep and was said to be able to accommodate up to 120 ships, 'without the trouble of shifting, mooring or unmooring any in the dock for taking in and out any other'. Looking at the illustration of the dock in 1717 (p.116) with 31 ships it is hard to imagine another 100 being allowed in, and if they were, they would certainly not get out again without a great deal of movement and jostling. However, it did its job well, for when the great storm of 1703 hit the Thames, many ships moored on the river suffered severe damage, while those in the dock all survived. It was very basic, without walls or warehouses, but surrounded on three sides by windbreaks. It was used mainly for fitting out East India Company ships, not for cargo.

Around the time of the illustration, the dock became home to a new trade, when a lease was taken out by the South Sea Company who would use it for their

The opening ceremony for St. Katharine's Dock in 1828.

St. Katharine's Dock today. Although the original buildings still exist, they have been hugely altered in conversion to apartments and pleasure boats now moor where once there were commercial craft.

whaling fleet, and established processing plants beside the dock to render down the blubber. The Company is best known for attracting vast numbers of investors, who lost everything when the company collapsed in what came to be known as the South Sea Bubble. But after the collapse, the dock continued to be used for whaling throughout the eighteenth century. It was this connection that resulted in the dock being renamed Greenland Dock.

As the whaling trade died away, the dock was sold to a London timber merchant, who added additional docks and timber pools, establishing the area as the main centre in London for imported timber – and it also became famous for the 'deal porters', who carried immense quantities of timber from ship to shore. An account published in the *New Survey of London Life and Labour* in 1929 gave a graphic account of the work:

Deal portering is heavy and dangerous work which cannot safely be undertaken by any save experienced men. The shoulder of an experienced deal porter is said to develop a callosity which enables it to bear the weight and friction of a load of planks. But even with a hardened shoulder the deal porter has an unenviable task. To carry over a shaking plankway a bundle of shaking slippery planks when a fall would almost certainly mean serious injury is work for specialists.

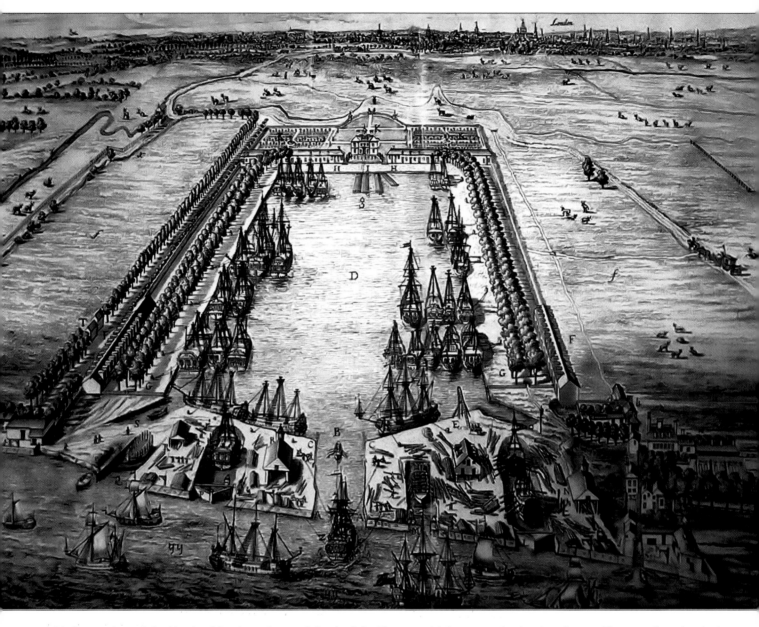

A bird's eye view of the Howland Dock on the south bank of the Thames with its protective barrier of trees. There are four dry docks on the riverbank.

The Greenland Dock was greatly extended at the end of the nineteenth century to cover 22½ acres, and the depth was increased to 31ft. This enabled large steamers to use the dock, and Cunard ran a service for cargo and passengers between here and the St. Lawrence River in Canada. By this time, it had become part of the Surrey Commercial Docks complex, with individual basins named after the areas they served, such as Canada Dock, Norway Dock and Russia Dock. Then, in 1909, they were all taken over by the Port of London Authority. We shall be looking at the development of the whole system under the new authority shortly.

All the docks we have been looking at so far were originally built in the age of sail, when steam was still something of a novelty. But the nineteenth century saw the position steadily reverse, with steamers dominating over sail, and with the change came the need to accommodate ever-larger vessels. This brought about a new period of dock development further down river specifically designed to handle steamships. The first was promoted and built by the same company that

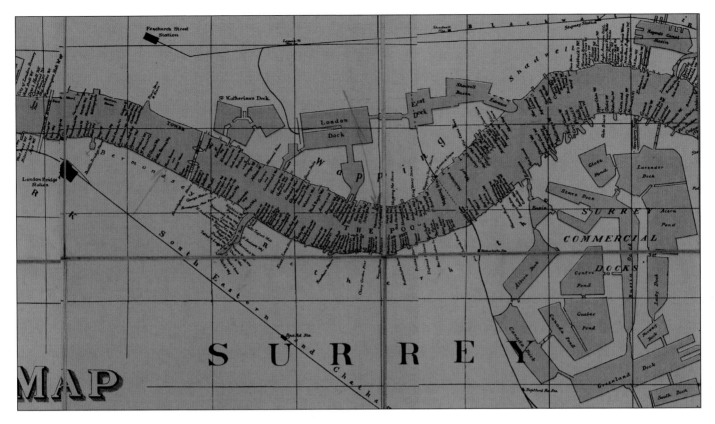

A map of the Thames from 1905, naming all the wharfs and docks between Tower Bridge and Bow Creek.

had built the St. Katharine's Dock, but with a new engineer in charge, George Parker Bidder. Opened in 1855, it was named the Victoria Dock, later changed to the Royal Victoria Dock. It was quite different from its predecessors in many ways, in size, layout and transport links. The main basin was roughly 3,000ft long and 1,000ft wide. Charles Dickens Jnr., son of the famous novelist, described the dock in detail in his *Dictionary of the Thames* 1881:

> The whole of the North Quay is furnished with jetties, eight in number altogether, four of which, reach upwards of 500 feet in length by about 150 in width, run boldly out into the very centre of the basin, affording accommodation on either side for the largest vessels yet afloat, or, as far as can be judged, likely at present to be afloat, or for two or more vessels of any ordinary size.

In the time between the construction of the St. Katharine's Dock and the Victoria Dock, a transport revolution had taken place in London, with the arrival of a complex railway system. One of the new lines that had reached the capital was the Eastern Counties & Thames Junction Railway and in 1846, it was extended down to a point on the Thames by the Woolwich ferry pier and named as the North Woolwich branch. The proposed entrance to the dock cut right across the line, so changes needed to be made. The original line now ended at the swing bridge by the lock and the railway was diverted round the north side of the complex. Direct connections were made with the quays, as Dickens again described:

> The whole of the quays traversed by a system of railway metals, from which sidings are carried off along either side of all the larger jetties, thus enabling goods to be hoisted straight out of the ship's hold into the truck whereon they are to be conveyed to their onward destination.

The other great improvement was the introduction of hydraulic cranes. Steam power was never much favoured in docks because of fire risks, and hydraulic cranes have no such problem. The jigger crane was invented by William Armstrong in Newcastle. Basically, this consists of the jigger, a

Building the Victoria – later Royal Victoria – Dock.

ram in a cylinder that is moved by water under high pressure. It is mounted to one side of the crane and is connected to the rope on the crane by a set of pulleys, which enable the short movement of the ram to be translated into a much longer movement to lift a load. Armstrong's other great invention was the hydraulic accumulator. This allowed water under pressure to be stored in a tower and just a short movement of a ram in the tower forces water at high pressure through a comparatively narrow pipe. The concept of hydraulics is something we experience every time we drive a car, when a comparatively light touch on the brake pedal compresses the hydraulic fluid and provides enough force to bring a heavy machine to a stop. Armstrong first applied the idea at Grimsby where he built an accumulator tower that dominates the harbour, rising to a height of 309ft. Because the cranes were only used intermittently, the accumulator could be used to store power and provide it only when it was actually needed. Victoria Docks were the

first to install hydraulics, but systems were soon in use in other London docks, not just for cranes but for moving devices such as swing bridges and lock gates. Fortunately, from the cost point of view, it was rapidly discovered that nothing on the scale of the Grimsby tower was actually needed.

It was soon apparent that even more dock space would be needed, and an extra dock was built alongside the Victoria, named inevitably the Albert Dock. Opened in 1880, the two docks were both given the added name of Royal. In many ways, the Royal Albert was similar to its predecessor and neighbour, but although it was longer it actually had a smaller overall area. Its construction created a problem that was turned to advantage. Once again, the entrance cut right across the line of the North Woolwich Railway. For a time, the engineers considered crossing the entrance with a swing bridge but decided that would create too great a problem for traffic both by rail and by water. So, the railway was sunk below the entrance

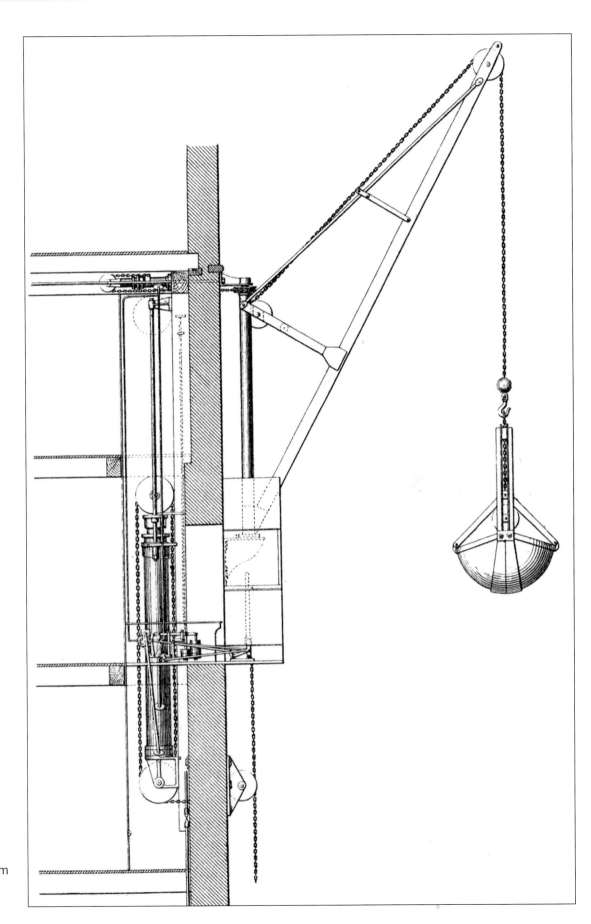

The introduction of hydraulic power to work machinery in the London docks was an important development. This illustration of 1887 shows a jigger crane, with the hydraulic ram on the left, working through pulleys.

in a tunnel, to re-emerge on the far side. The main line of the Branch now circled to the north of the docks, providing the ideal opportunity to provide sidings down to the quayside.

Traffic continued to grow, and in 1886 a new dock was built further down the river at Tilbury. The site was selected partly because the railway had already reached what was then called Tilbury Fort to connect with the local ferry service. The choice was to have long term implications for the whole story of London's dockland.

The new docks might have been an improvement in terms of mechanisation, but the working life of the dock workers had scarcely changed for centuries. They were basically divided into two groups, dockers who unloaded ships and stevedores who loaded them. The latter's work was crucial, particularly in the days of sail. Cargo had to be stowed with care, ensuring it was well balanced and secured. If the ship was caught in bad weather and cargo came loose then it could end in tragedy. But dockers and stevedores alike were casual labourers, hired by the job, with no guarantee of work

from one day to the next. The system was complex. When a ship was to be loaded, for example, there would be a number of master stevedores competing for the job. Once a master had agreed a price with the owner, he would set about employing gangs of men to do the actual work. There would be crowds waiting each morning hoping to be chosen – usually in small gangs used to working together, often based on family ties. The master stevedore wanted the job done efficiently, but the less he had to pay in wages, the greater his profit. It was far from unknown to hire fewer men than were really needed and then, if they seemed to be falling behind, call in one or two who had not been given anything that morning to put in perhaps just a couple of hours. The same system operated with the dockers. It was degrading as one docker described it:

We are driven into a shed, iron-barred from end to end, outside of which a foreman or contractor walks up and down with the air of a dealer in a cattlemarket, picking and choosing from a crowd of men, who, in

Tilbury Dock with the rolling lift bridge opening to allow a vessel to pass.

Thanks to refrigeration, perishables could be brought to London from the other side of the world; unloading frozen meat.

their eagerness to obtain employment, trample each other under foot, and where like beasts they fight for the chances of a day's work.

Those words were written by Ben Tillet who in 1898 was to lead action against the employers, by calling a strike. The immediate cause was the decision by the East and West India Dock Company to cut the 'plus' money paid for getting a job finished ahead of time. But they also demanded the pay for workers should be increased from fivepence to sixpence an hour. They at once received the support of the stevedores, and soon other workers, such as the lightermen, joined in. The port was paralysed. The employers' response was immediate, claiming that any advance in wages would reduce the dividends paid to shareholders and drive shipping from the port. The Chairman of the Dock Directors said in an interview, 'When the pinch comes as it must, the hopes

of the strikers will receive a severe shock and I shall be surprised if there is any backbone left.' He was to be proved wrong.

The strike had begun in early August, but it was always going to be a struggle. The strikers had no resources to fall back on and money soon began to run out. Support came from an unexpected source. Australian dock workers raised over £30,000 for the strikers and their families. 'The pinch' the employers had expected had been averted. The situation called for immediate action and the Lord Mayor of London formed a Mansion House Committee, chaired by the Catholic Cardinal Manning. The two sides got together and the employers conceded almost all the workers' demands, notably the increase from five to six pence an hour. On 16 September, everyone was back at work.

After the strike, the various dock groups got together to form a single Union. Although they had won the

Loading railway carriages for Rhodesia – now Zimbabwe – at the Royal Docks.

strike, conditions remained far from perfect. The casual system still remained in force, and the numbers of men employed at any one time fluctuated wildly. The *Board of Trade Labour Gazette* published figures that the greatest number employed in the docks on a single day in 1913 was 18,228 and the smallest 11,164. There were other changes that affected the workforce. Tom Mann, writing in 1910, described how that introduction of grain elevators had reduced the size of the workforce:

A very moderate statement is that two men out of every three employed in the discharge of grain are now dispensed with, i.e. thrown into the ranks of the unemployed. The system now resorted to is to have as few handling of cargo as possible. Thus at the Victoria Docks there are two flour mills. The grain is hauled in at one side of the mill from the vessel or lighter, and it goes through all the necessary processes almost without the aid of the man. It is then lowered as flour from the other side of the mill into the barge ready for delivery.

Mechanisation may have taken away some jobs, but trade was still increasing and ships were getting even larger. It was time for another dock to be constructed. Work on the King George V Dock was begun in 1912 by the Port of London Authority, but the outbreak of war brought everything to a halt for four years. It was completed in 1921 and was able to berth the largest ships of the day. There were improvements throughout the docks, with the introduction of electricity for lighting and for operating cranes. Refrigeration meant meat could be

A pair of narrow boats alongside a cargo ship in Limehouse basin.

imported from abroad and became an important part of the trade of the docks. Industrial relations continued to deteriorate throughout the country, culminating in the General Strike of May 1926, in which the dockers joined a million and a half or more workers who came out to support the miners. They picketed the dock area, but on 8 May, trucks arrived with an army escort, passed through the picket lines and filled up with food. Another major problem was the lack of electricity, which meant food in the refrigerated areas was going to go bad. The Navy supplied two submarines, who used their generators to fix the problem. Four days later the strike was called off.

There was far worse to come for all dock workers when the Second World War began in September 1939. The docks were obvious targets for German raids. On 7 September 1940, it was recorded that 348 bombers with

an escort of 617 fighters appeared over London and one of their main targets was the Royal Docks Group. It was not just the docks themselves that were damaged, but homes in the area were also hit, with 146 locals killed. Many who survived, lost their homes and many of them were taken to temporary accommodation at a school in Canning Town. Buses were supposed to have been sent to take the homeless families to safety, but thanks to a mix up they went to Camden Town instead. By the time the mistake had been recognised, the school had been hit. Official figures for deaths were 73, but it was generally thought there were far more casualties.

The post war years were to see further changes throughout the docks. In 1947, the Government set up the National Dock Labour Board, which registered dockers and provided them with 'fall back' money, when no work was available. But it was to be many years before the

The King George V Dock at its busiest in the early years of the twentieth century.

Billowing smoke rising high over London's Dockland during the Blitz, 1940-1.

A Heinkel bomber over the Surrey Docks during a raid in the Second World War.

casual labour system came to an end. By then, however, the trade was already declining. The killer blow came with the development of containerisation. This required new technology and the new generation of container ships were too large for the journey upriver. Tilbury was already a busy port but now it was to be converted by the Port of London Authority into a specialist container port at a cost of £30 million. It was completed in 1967. The old London docks could no longer compete and it was decided to close down all commercial operations. The last ship left on 7 December 1981. A vital part of London's story had come to an end.

The modern container port at Tilbury. The modernisation on this site led to the closure of the commercial docks upriver.

London's Dockland is now a busy commercial centre of towering office blocks, but the old life of the docks is still remembered with this statue by L.S. Johnson at the Royal Victoria Dock.

CHAPTER 7

SAVING LIVES

Think of lifeboats, and London and the Thames are not the first places that come to mind. We tend to think of them as being launched from coastal stations to dash away to save lives at sea. Indeed, for most of the history of the lifeboat service that is where lifeboats were stationed and that is what they did. But London has played a vital role in the story as well.

Long before there was any official lifeboat organisation and before there were even any special lifeboats, local communities around the coast would set out in their own boats to help rescue vessels in trouble. Conditions that could wreck ships were just as likely to put the rescuers at risk of their own lives and by the end of the eighteenth century, there were attempts to build what were, in theory at least, self-righting lifeboats. An early version was designed by Lionel Lukin in 1787,

by adapting an existing type of fishing boat common in North East England, the coble. Two years later, in a competition, another vessel was designed, this time by William Woodhave of South Shields, again based on the coble, and lined with cork. Although his design did not win the competition, it was the basis for the first purpose-built lifeboat constructed by Henry Greathead. It was the basis for lifeboat design for many years, powered by oars and sails.

The first official Institution for rescue at sea was established at Liverpool in 1773 but seems to have taken a pessimistic view of the prospect of rescue, as it was named 'The Liverpool Institution for Recovering Drowned Persons'. It was to be another fifty years before an organisation for saving lives rather than recovering corpses was formed. The driving force

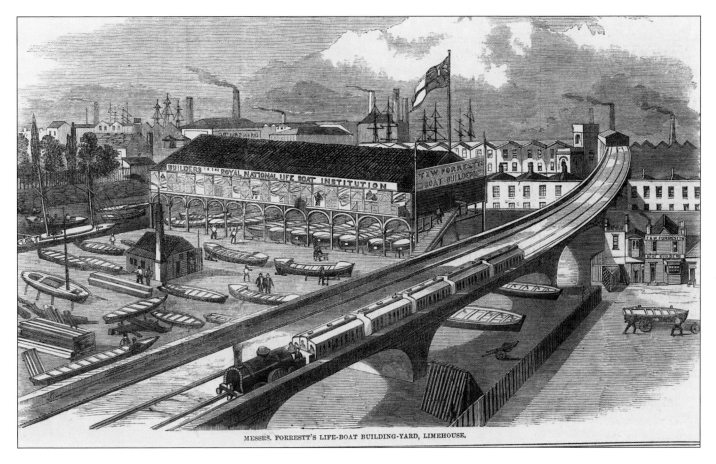

MESSRS. FORRESTT'S LIFE-BOAT BUILDING-YARD, LIMEHOUSE.

The Forrestt yard was an important builder of lifeboats for the RNLI in the nineteenth century.

behind it was Sir William Hillary, former equerry to the Duke of Sussex. After his retirement to the Isle of Man, he began promoting the idea of a national lifeboat service, and the result was the formation of the National Institution for the Preservation of Life from Shipwreck in 1824 with King George IV as patron. It would later change its name to the Royal National Lifeboat Institution (RNLI). In the 1850s, another competition was launched to find the best design and standardise lifeboat construction. The resulting shape will be familiar to anyone attending a lifeboat station – preserved in the familiar collecting box. The vessels were known as 'pulling and sailing', simply meaning that they could be both rowed and sailed. One of the most important shipyards to be given a contract to build for the RNLI was Forrestt & Son who had a yard at Limehouse. They continued building lifeboats and testing them in the Limehouse cut until the 1880s, when the company relocated to Wivenhoe.

The pulling and sailing lifeboats were the only lifeboats available for most of the nineteenth century.

Sir William Hillary was the first to suggest that the RNLI should investigate the possibility of developing steam lifeboats. The advantages of steam had been shown at several stations, where steam tugs had been used to tow the lifeboats out to sea in very bad weather conditions. A grant of £600 from the International Fisheries Exhibition was put towards developing ideas for a new lifeboat. A committee was set up in 1888, which included John Thorneycroft, who had already developed a reputation for innovation in the steam world. But it was a model sent in by the J. & F. Green shipyard of Blackwall that was to be the basis for full trials. Instead of a propeller, the boats were moved hydraulically, by pumping water at high pressure out through ducts below the waterline. The first of the class to be built at the Green's yard was the *Duke of Northumberland,* named after a former president of the RNLI, a fifty-foot steel vessel, capable of a top speed of almost 10 knots. She went into service at Harwich in September 1890.

Green's built two more water jet vessels, but the next three steam lifeboats were more conventionally driven

The RNLI's first steam powered lifeboat *Duke of Northumberland.*

by propeller and were built in East Cowes. The three water jet vessels remained in service for over forty years and between them saved 570 lives. There was, however, one tragedy in 1900, when one of the propeller craft, the *James Stewart No. 4*, was wrecked off Padstow with the loss of eight crew. No more steam lifeboats were built after that. In the twentieth century, the diesel engine became the main source of power as it remains today. That might have brought an end to London's connection with the RNLI. The new connection followed another tragic accident.

On 19 August 1989, the pleasure steamer *Marchioness* was hired for a birthday party that went on well into the night and the early hours of the next day. She was heading downstream against the tide at about quarter to two in the morning, with 130 on board, when she was hit in the stern by the dredger *Bowbelle* travelling at speed. The *Marchioness* was turned sideways by the blow, pushed under the dredger's bows and sank. Fifty-one of those on the pleasure steamer died. Although, it was generally agreed that if a proper lookout had been maintained, the accident could have been avoided, there was never a successful prosecution of any of those involved. But one result of the subsequent enquiry was a request from the government for the RNLI to establish a lifeboat station on the Thames.

The Tower Station was opened at the beginning of 2002 at the pier close to the Tower of London. It was then moved to its present location at the old Waterloo Police Pier but has kept its original name. Unlike the vast majority of British lifeboat stations, it is permanently manned 24 hours a day with a professional crew, though

London's Tower lifeboat station is one of the country's busiest and is permanently manned.

volunteers also work alongside them. Between them they cover 16 miles of river between Barking Creek and Battersea. They average almost 500 launches a year and have literally saved hundreds of lives. A second lifeboat station was established at the same time at Chiswick, but unlike Tower is entirely run by volunteers. They cover the upper part of the tidal Thames from Battersea to Richmond. They are able to reach any part of their stretch within a quarter of an hour. Just as the steam lifeboats were faster than the rowing lifeboats, so the new boats are twice as fast again.

The other institution famous for saving lives at sea is Trinity House, best known for its work in controlling the lighthouses of England, Wales and Northern Ireland. Yet, surprisingly once again, there is a very significant London connection. In 1803, Trinity acquired a plot of land at Blackwall, where they built storehouses for buoys and seamarks. Showing remarkable foresight, they invited Michael Faraday to come and carry out experiments on site and provided him with a workshop. He had been the first to demonstrate how an electric current could be generated by moving a conductor in a magnetic field – the basis of the electric generator. He set out to see if he could provide a better light than anything then available by using electricity. The electric light bulb had yet to be invented, but Humphry Davy had demonstrated the carbon arc lamp. Basically, this consisted of two carbon rods, attached to a source of electric current. The rods were brought together, creating a discharge through the air. They were then gradually moved apart, and the tips of the carbon rods became very hot. The carbon vapourised, emitting a bright, white

The experimental lighthouse used to test new lights and lenses on one end of the buoy warehouse on the Trinity House wharf.

light. Faraday experimented with arc lamps, powered by batteries, in the 1850s, and though they produced satisfactory lights, controlling them was difficult and the batteries gave out noxious fumes, which would have been decidedly unhealthy in the confined spaces of a lighthouse. Faraday produced a much more satisfactory version when, instead of batteries, he used a generator, powered by a steam engine. Two versions were installed, one at Dungeness and the second at South Foreland. But electric lighting was not really developed for lighthouse use until the twentieth century. Faraday did, however, provide one very useful device, a chimney that could be fitted to remove the fumes from the old style lanterns, to prevent fogging the glass and reducing the power of the light.

When James Douglas became chief engineer for Trinity House in 1862, he organised a new building programme at Blackwall that included constructing a lighthouse tower specifically for experimenting with new forms of lighting. This was an octagonal brick structure with an octagonal lantern on top, set at one end of the buoy warehouse. There was originally another lantern, set on the opposite end of the warehouse, but that no longer exists, though it can be seen in a photograph in the 1920s. The site was first used for experiments in March 1869. A group of observers gathered on Charlton Hill, on the far side of the river, to observe the differences between white light emitted from one lantern and red light, passed through ruby glass, from the other. They were hoping to work out how to use alternating red and white flashes as an identification signal for the new lighthouse planned for Bell Rock. There were to be more experiments with different lenses and later better forms of electric lighting over the years. It finally closed in 1988 when the site was

The nineteenth century cargo steamer *Robin* now has a permanent berth beside the old Trinity House wharf.

sold and is now an active arts centre. The site has also become home to a remarkable survivor. The steam ship *Robin* was built nearby at the Orchard House Yard on Bow Creek and launched in 1890. She is the last surviving example of a cargo steamer built in the Victorian era. Though supplied with an up-to-date triple expansion steam engine, with three cylinders, she also was rigged as a schooner with sails on three masts. It is hoped that the site will be home to other preserved vessels in the future.

Completing a trilogy of life saving organisations, it is time to look at the London Fire Brigade and its fire boats. The idea of fighting fires from a specialised boat on the river dates back long before the formation of an official fire brigade. In the eighteenth century, fire engines

The *Massey Shaw* at work fighting a great fire at a Wapping warehouse.

were run by independent insurance companies, and the first recorded fire boat was ordered by the Sun Fire Assurance Company of London in 1765. It was rowed and carried a hand-operated pump. The advantages of such vessels for fighting fires along the waterfront or in ships are obvious, not the least of which being the availability of an unlimited supply of water for the pumps. The fire boats, however, really came into their own in the latter part of the nineteenth century with the formation of the Metropolitan Fire Brigade in 1866 under the direction of Captain Eyre Massey Shaw. He at once set about replacing the old horse-drawn fire engines for the streets with steam-powered engines, and also introduced steam fire boats.

There is no better way to illustrate the role of these craft than to look at the history of one vessel, named after the former head of the service, the *Massey Shaw*. By the time she was built in 1935, at J. Samuel Whites on

the Isle of Wight, steam power had given way to diesel. She is powered by two powerful 8-cylinder engines and her twin pumps each supply water under pressure at a rate of 1,500 gallons a minute. Within a year of launching, the vessel had played a role in quelling a massive fire at Colonial Wharf, Wapping where it was estimated she helped save £1 million worth of goods. But the boat's finest hours came in the Second World War. In 1940, she was part of the flotilla that went to Dunkirk with a volunteer crew and brought back over 500 troops. Back home, the fire boats all had a vital role to play during the Blitz. There were times when due to bomb damage, water sources on the shore were simply not working, and the fire boats were invaluable. Of the fleet that worked through the war, one was sunk by a bomb, but the *Massey Shaw* survived. In 1947, she was given a refit with the addition of a permanent wooden wheelhouse and was soon back in service. In 1950, she was called to

The preserved firefighting vessel *Massey Shaw*.

a huge fire at a margarine warehouse but a decade later she was put on the reserve list as more modern craft took over the work. She was decommissioned in 1971 and that could have seen her end up like so many old vessels, heading for scrap. However, a volunteer society was formed to preserve and restore the historic vessel and in 1982 she was presented to them on a fifty-year lease. Now the vessel is fully restored and has a home in West India Docks, but is regularly to be seen out on the river for special occasions. Today, the fire brigade has two fire boats moored at Lambeth. They are both considerably faster than their predecessors, with a top speed of 30 knots. They remain an important part of the London fire service, typically launching around 150 times a year, not just to fight fires, but to help tow vessels in distress and helping the RNLI in rescue operations. They are still very much part of the working life of the Thames.

Although originally formed to save property, not lives, the river police have nevertheless over the years been involved in many life-saving operations. The story begins at the end of the eighteenth century when merchants were losing vast quantities of valuable goods from ships in the Thames. A group of men got together to find ways of combating this wholesale pilfering and theft. They were the Glasgow Merchant Patrick Colquhoun, who had made a fortune in the tobacco trade with the West Indies, a former master mariner and Justice of the Peace, John Harriot, and the philosopher Jeremy Bentham. They proposed establishing a Marine Police Force and with government approval and an initial grant of £4,200 from the merchants who had business on the river, a one-year trial began in 1798.

The new force had its headquarters at Wapping, with five surveyors who patrolled the river day and night, rowed in galleys by police watermen. Four more surveyors with attendant constables oversaw ships being loaded and unloaded, while a third group patrolled the quays. The operation was successful – too successful as far as the professional thieves were concerned and those dockers who had been used to adding to their income at the expense of the merchants. A mob of around 2,000 men attempted to burn down the Wapping police station with the men inside. They were repulsed but one constable lost his life in the fight. In spite of this event, the force thrived, and Colquhoun began lobbying to have the force become an official body, supported by public funds. In 1800, parliament passed an Act to establish the Thames River Police. Two other police stations were established in the 1820s at Waterloo and Blackfriars. In 1839, they amalgamated with the Metropolitan Police Service as the Thames Division. They continue to this day, patrolling the river as they have for more than two centuries. In 2001, they received a new name, the Marine Policing Unit. Their headquarters is now back where it all began in Wapping.

CHAPTER 8

THE PRESENT DAY

The greatest changes have obviously come in the old dock areas, which have been redeveloped. Old warehouses have been converted and are now fashionable apartment blocks. Office towers surround what was once a stretch of water crowded with ships and barges. The change began in 1980 with the creation of the London Docklands Development Corporation, followed two years later by the creation of an Urban Enterprise Zone on the Isle of Dogs. This was to become the Canary Wharf development. The name originally derived from the fact that it was where ships from the Canary Islands unloaded their cargoes, but 'canary' is also the name for a sweet wine, and, given the proliferation of wine bars in the area, is quite appropriate. It is now a financial centre to rival the old centre in the City.

Most of the working boats have left the Thames now, and many of the old barges have been converted into houseboats. But one watery trade still survives. There are still passenger boats on the river. The difference between the boats of today and those of earlier generations is that where, in the past, they were an essential part of London's traffic and the best and quickest way of getting from one part of the city to another, today they are mostly used simply for pleasure trips. Before the arrival of the railways, steamers were used to take visitors to the seaside resorts on the south coast. But once the line from London to Brighton, for example, was opened in 1841 it was far quicker to get to the seaside by train than it was by boat – and no chance of getting seasick. There were, however, a number of vessels that left London on longer excursions, taking passengers across the Channel to view the French coast. One of these motor vessels was the *Royal Daffodil,* that went into service in April 1939, sailing from Tower Pier. She was requisitioned for war service in 1939 and was among the craft used for the

The waterfront at Wapping: most of the former warehouses have now been converted into apartments.

With the closure of the commercial docks, the Isle of Dogs was transformed into a financial centre – Canary Wharf by night.

evacuation of Dunkirk and rescued 9,500 men in seven trips. After the war she resumed her sailings to France from either Gravesend or Tilbury and from 1957 to 1963, she enjoyed an exotic if noisy life as a music centre, featuring several of the rock and roll stars of the age. She was scrapped in 1967.

The motor vessel *Royal Daffodil* ran excursions from Tower Pier after a distinguished wartime career that included taking part in the Dunkirk evacuation.

But although few foreign trips were made, the steamers did continue to run up and down the river and though steam has been replaced by diesel, they still do today. Trips from the centre down to Greenwich or up to Richmond are always popular. They still offer unique chances to enjoy the rich variety of the river and its surroundings and the trips are usually accompanied by an excellent and often highly entertaining commentary. My first London job was in a laboratory at Chiswick, and in summer it was very pleasant to walk down to a riverside pub and sit outside with a pint and a sandwich. And every day, the same trip boat would pass on its way upstream, and through the loudspeaker you could clearly hear the same words: 'If you look over to your right you can see the drunks outside The City Barge'. And we would raise our glasses in salute. Modern vessels on the river can offer rather more to passengers, though whether one prefers the new or the older approach is a matter of personal taste. *Avontuur IV* 'built in the Netherlands' is typical of the new approach. It has a main saloon, a licensed bar and a dance floor complete with DJ equipment as well as a more conventional open upper deck.

A new service of river buses was inaugurated in 1999, known as Thames Clippers. They offered a high-speed commuter service. In 2020, the company was rebranded as Uber Boats. They offer a regular service, leaving at twenty minute intervals between Westminster and Woolwich Arsenal Pier as well as pleasure trips that go between Woolwich and Putney. The latest boats on the run are catamarans.

The pleasure cruiser *Avontuur IV* offers a wide variety of entertainment on its regular trips on the Thames.

The new fast Uber boat service offers a regular service along the Thames with stops along the way.

One major change to the river came as a result of an event in 1953, when a tidal surge from the North Sea flooded much of the estuary. To prevent such sudden tidal surges reaching further up the river and flooding parts of central London, a committee proposed that a flood barrier should be built. Several designs were put forward, and finally reduced to just two schemes. The final decision was taken by Sir Hermann Bondi, an interesting choice as his best-known work was in astrophysics rather than engineering. The most interesting features of the chosen design were the gates that could be opened to allow shipping through and closed when necessary. Instead of lifting vertically, they rotate around a horizontal axis. Their inventor, Charles Draper, is said to have got the idea from an unlikely source – the taps on his cooker. The four large central

steel gates weigh 3,700 tonnes each. Work began in 1974 on a site near Woolwich and was completed ten years later. Since then, the barrier has, at the time of writing, been closed almost two hundred times. As well as helping to keep London dry, the barrier has also become a tourist attraction and is the second largest flood barrier in the world.

The changes in London's rivers and canals have been dramatic, but it is still possible to enjoy reminders of a long and fascinating history through preserved craft and museums. And there are still glimpses to be had of buildings and structures that have their own story to tell, especially in the region downstream from Tower Bridge, as the photograph of Wapping below vividly demonstrates. And the best way to do that is, as it has been for centuries, is to travel the Thames by boat.

The imposing Thames
flood barrier.

Warehouse and pub at
Wapping.

PLACES TO VISIT AND PRESERVED CRAFT

Museums

London Canal Museum, New Wharf Road, N1 9RT, canalmuseum.org.uk

London Transport Museum, Covent Garden Piazza, WC2e 7BB, ltmuseum.co.uk

Museum of London Docklands, No.1 Warehouse, West India Quay, E14 4AL museumoflondon.org.uk/museum-london-docklands

National Maritime Museum, Park Row, Greenwich, SE10 9, rmg.co.uk/national-maritime-museum

Thames River Police Museum, Wapping Police Station, Wapping High Street, E1w 2NE, thamespolicemuseum.org.uk

Trinity Buoy Wharf, 64 Orchard Place, E14 0JW, trinitybuoywharf.com

Preserved Craft

HMS *Belfast*, The Queen's Walk, SE1 2JH, iwm.org.uk/hms-belfast

Cutty Sark, King William Walk, Greenwich, SE10 9HT, rmg.co.uk/cutty-sark

Massey Shaw fire boat, West India Docks, E14, masseyshaw.org

ST *Portwey* steam tug, South Quay, West India Docks, E 14, stportwey.co.uk

SS *Robin*, Trinity Buoy Wharf (as above), ssrobin.com

PS *Tattershall Castle* paddle steamer/pub, Victoria Embankment, SW1A 2HR, thetattershallcastle.co.uk

FURTHER READING

Banbury, Philip, *Shipbuilders of the Thames and Medway*, 1971

Beilby, Alec, *Heroes All! The Story of the RNLI*, 1992

Burton, Anthony, *The Rise and Fall of British Shipbuilding* (2nd ed.), 2013

Burton, Anthony and Pratt, Derek, *Britain's Canals*, 2020

Carr, Frank G.G., *Sailing Barges*, 1971

Craig, Robin, *The Ship: Steam Tramps and Cargo Liners*, 1981

Greenhill, Basil, *The Ship: The Life and Death of the Merchant Sailing Ship*, 1980

Hovey, John, *A Tale of Two Ports*, 1990

Macdougall, Philip, *Royal Dockyards*, 1983

Pratt, Derek, *London's Waterways*, 2010

Tucker, Joan, *Ferries of the Lower Thames*, 2010

ACKNOWLEDGEMENTS

The author would like to thank the following for providing illustrations. Acabashi 137; Alan Binns, 8, Andy Duingley, 90, Ben Brackshaw, 124 (top), Ben Willacott, 52 (top), Biblioteca, 63, Bodleian, 73 (bottom),British Library, 18, British Museum, 14, C. McGlee, 30; Canal & Riverside, 139; Chris McKenna, 30, Christian Bortes – delete (Picture was omitted), City of London, 54, Clem Rutter, 126 (top), Derek Pratt, 83, Dietner Rabich, 135, G.D. Evans, 21, Geni. 15, Gordon Joli, 125, Ham II, 34 [this is a new entry], Hul and East Riding, 144, Indiscenti, 50, 52, ICE, 119, Illustrated London News, 47, 130, Imperial War Museum, 125. James Gray, 124 (bottom), Joan Tucker, 48, John Benjamin Stone, 138, John Linwood, 8, John Meredith, 52 (bottom), 92, 120, 122, 123; Kaki, 50, King of Hearts, 136(top), Mary Rose, 23, 26, Massey Shaw, 132, 133, Masters & Fellows, 20, 22, Miss Wain, 68, Musee Bayeux, 16, Museum of English Rural Lie, 24; Museum of London,23, 26, 41, 42, 51, 114, NMM, 31, 32, 33, 41, 42, 51, 57 (bottom), 111, New York Times Bureau, 104, Oxfordshire, 77; Peter Trimming, 115, PM History, 52, Serocat, 129, Steve Sea, Thacker, 107, WAG, 64 (top), 66 (top), 67, 69, 70, 72, 73 (top), 75, 76, 80, 82, 194; Yarrow, 105.

INDEX